G000154032

During the last five years Paulet... helped many thousands of p... problems of a variety of eatin... eating, bulimia nervosa, food... through her work at the Mais... hensive and effective programme of treatment based on personal counselling, relaxation therapy and re-education of nutrition and eating habits is described in her previously published *The Food Trap*.

The individual-oriented approach she devised aims to help break the vicious circle of an eating disorder but it is not an easy process, requiring commitment and perseverance. The excuses are numerous and Paulette Maisner has heard them often: 'I've no time', 'it's boring', 'special occasions make it impossible', 'I'm a vegetarian'. In response to these excuses, and in answer to the common question 'What *can* I eat?', she has written *Excuses Won't Cure You*.

Detailed here is the *Eating Plan*, a simple but effective method of changing poor eating habits, integral to the success of treatment. Covering all eventualities, a wide selection of foods – with recipes – is given, plus the relevant explanations of why you should steer clear of certain 'trigger' foods that can cause binges.

Designed to provide the practical information that will encourage success, *Excuses Won't Cure You* is an excellent source of advice and support for anyone wishing to change the destructive pattern of bad eating habits.

EXCUSES WON'T CURE YOU

Previous Publications

THE FOOD TRAP (with Rosemary Turner)
FEASTING AND FASTING (with Jenny Pulling)

The Maisner Centre
PO Box 464
Hove
East Sussex BN3 2BN
Tel. Brighton 0273 729818

Details of your local branch of the Centre and the postal
courses available can be obtained by sending a large
stamped, addressed envelope to the above address.

EXCUSES WON'T CURE YOU

An effective self-help approach to changing your eating habits

PAULETTE MAISNER
with ALISON CRIDLAND

UNWIN PAPERBACKS
London   Sydney

First published in Great Britain by Unwin ® Paperbacks,
an imprint of Unwin Hyman Limited, in 1987

Copyright © Paulette Maisner and Alison Cridland 1987

All rights reserved. No part of this publication may be reproduced,
stored in a retrieval system, or transmitted in any form or by any
means, electronic, mechanical, photocopying, recording or otherwise,
without the prior permission of Unwin Hyman Limited

UNWIN HYMAN LIMITED
Denmark House, 37–39 Queen Elizabeth Street, London SE1 2QB
and 40 Museum Street, London WC1A 1LU

Allen & Unwin Australia Pty Ltd
8 Napier Street, North Sydney, NSW 2060, Australia

Unwin Paperbacks with the Port Nicholson Press,
60 Cambridge Terrace, Wellington, New Zealand

British Library Cataloguing in Publication Data

Maisner, Paulette
    Excuses won't cure you: an effective
    self-help approach to changing your
    eating habits.
1. Appetite disorders—Treatment
I. Title II. Cridland, Alison
616.85'2   RC552.A72

ISBN 0-04-613069-1

Typeset in 10 on 11 point Palatino by Pentacor, High Wycombe,
and printed by the Guernsey Press, Guernsey, Channel Islands.

Acknowledgements

Permission has been given to reproduce recipes from the following publications:

THE FARM VEGETARIAN COOKBOOK by Louise Hagler
Published by The Book Publishing Company, 1978

THE ST IVEL COOKBOOK

THE SAINSBURY BOOK OF SLIMMING by Rhona Newman
Published by Cathay Books, 1980

THE NEW COOKBOOK by Miriam Polunin
Published by Macdonald & Co., London, 1984

THE 60-MINUTE COOKBOOK by Pamela Westland
Published by Book Club Associates, London, 1980

THE LOW BLOOD SUGAR COOKBOOK by Francyne Davis
Published by Bantam Books, U.S.A., 1973

LOW, SLOW, DELICIOUS by Martha Lomask
Published by Book Club Associates, London, 1980

The author would like to thank the individuals concerned for their co-operation.

*To Gary who won in spite of
everything and with special thanks
to Christie for all the help and
support over the past years.*

Contents

Introduction

The Eating Plan contained in this book is used at the Maisner Centre in Hove, England. It has helped thousands of compulsive eaters, mainly women but increasingly more men too, to get their eating under control. They have come from all over the country, from the north of Scotland to the south of England and also overseas, for help. Children from as young as 12 to 84-year-old pensioners, people from all walks of life, the unemployed to a leading barrister, housewives to doctors, shop girls to accountants, have been shown how to control their addiction to food by following the plan.

The plan is a simple, yet effective way of getting your eating back to normal for good. It suggests a wide selection of food which you should eat and explains clearly why you should steer clear of other foods which may cause binges. The Eating Plan has been slightly amended from my previous book, *The Food Trap*, as I am constantly updating the advice to compulsive eaters through feedback from clients who have successfully got their eating habits under control.

This book was written, first, because I found myself and my staff constantly repeating the same answers to the same never-ending excuses from clients explaining why they could not stick to the Eating Plan: from 'lack of money' to 'being a vegetarian' or 'because it is nearly Christmas', and secondly to answer the constant pleas from clients 'what on earth can I eat?'

EXCUSES WON'T CURE YOU

1 The right approach

There is a way out of the Food Trap. The Eating Plan has helped thousands of compulsive eaters to overcome their problems and be free of their addiction to food. But it is hard work, there is no magic cure.

There are physical and psychological causes of compulsive eating. In many cases those who suffer find themselves drawn, unawares, into the downward spiral of feasting and fasting. Unlike drug addicts who have plenty of warning about the fatal effects of drugs before they make the decision to take the first fix, compulsive eaters are caught in the Eating Trap, addicted and obsessed with food, without anyone spelling out the danger.

The media constantly encourages you to diet, while at the same time enticing you to partake of sugary snacks and sweets in between meals. No one explains how diets claiming to produce rapid weight loss actually affect your body *and* your mind. Drastically reducing calorie-intake is not only nutritionally dangerous; it also triggers the body's natural defence mechanism which resists any dramatic weight loss by burning calories more slowly – it is nature's way of surviving a famine. This leaves you feeling deprived and resentful, trying to stick to your diet only to discover you have not lost any weight. Result – you feel despair . . . and binge.

With the help of the Eating Plan set out in this book it is possible to overcome the physical effects of your eating disorder. In most instances this will also mean confronting the psychological problems at the same time. Many compulsive eaters say: 'I only binge when I'm bored,' 'I only binge when I'm angry,' 'I only binge when I'm tired,' or 'I only binge when I'm depressed.' They recognise that they have an eating problem, and even the psychological root of that problem, but fail to face up to it because they cannot see an *easy* answer.

The Eating Plan outlines which foods will help you to get your eating under control and how they do this. It also highlights which foods to avoid and why. Follow the Eating Plan and your blood sugar will be stabilised, you will feel less depressed, you will have more energy and you will be able to think clearly about your lifestyle. This will give you the opportunity to find the way out of the Food Trap, and away from the binger's world of confusion, indecision and misery.

While many compulsive eaters are prepared to take a remedy for a cold or seek medical treatment for a broken arm, they are not prepared to take action to solve the major illness which can be ruining their lives – compulsive eating. Often they will find a stream of excuses to avoid following the Eating Plan and getting better. Janice did not have the time because she was having her kitchen decorated; Suzanne could not afford to because she first had to save up for a new outfit for a wedding, and Katie said it was nearly Christmas so she might as well binge . . . and so on.

Although they hate living in despair, some compulsive eaters do not *want* to get well. A few use their eating disorder as emotional blackmail against their families, watching their parents, husband and children feel guilty and helpless. Others use it as an excuse for the problems in their lives, perhaps they are lonely, in an unhappy marriage or a boring job. Once their eating is under control what will they have left to blame for their unhappiness? Penny told us she was starting a new job, but, in the same breath, added: 'I may have to give it up if it is too stressful. I am bulimic and I have to be careful what I do.' Her problem is not food; it is that she cannot face up to the stress of work. Jackie said: 'I cannot make friends because I am a compulsive eater.' Jackie needs to build up her confidence then she would make friends.

The first step you have to take if you really want to overcome your compulsive eating is to adopt a *positive* attitude. Too often compulsive eaters allow themselves to hide behind a cloud of negativism; Sally was addicted to chocolate digestive biscuits and would binge on several packets at a time. We tried to persuade her to stop buying them. She replied 'I cannot do that because my dog is addicted to them too.' On the other hand Lucy, who was also addicted to chocolate digestives, said she would make an effort to give them up: 'My dog is getting fat because I feed them to him too and I don't want him to suffer because of my weakness.'

Madeline's son died tragically while she was trying to solve her eating problem. She told us she felt there was no point in making an effort to get well. 'My son is dead, there is no reason for me to get better now.'

Shelley also faced a traumatic time when her daughter died as she was tackling her eating problem. Shelley told us: 'I am determined to get well now for the sake of my other children and my husband. I must get my eating under control to be able to cope with my daughter's death.'

Emma, a university student, said there was no point in trying to get her eating under control before her final exams – 'I am going to fail my exams anyway and then I won't get a job and I'll have to go on the dole.' Another student, Tina, told us she was determined to get her eating problem solved before her finals. 'Even if I fail my exams at least I will have gained something, my eating will be back to normal again. And with that problem solved I am sure it will be much easier to face re-sitting my exams next year.'

The key is that if you *want* to get well, you can. Having said that, it is also important to remember that there is no easy way out of the Food Trap. Take a look in the mirror. You probably think that you are over-weight; you lack confidence and feel guilty, ashamed and unhappy about your eating. If you are bulimic and force yourself to be sick after a binge you may have bloodshot eyes and an unsightly protruding stomach. Compulsive eaters tend to be very caring people but in the grips of their problem many become selfish and boring. Are you self-obsessed, weighing yourself every day, thinking of how you will look and how life will change for the better when you reach that mythical 'ideal' weight? In the past you may have reached your goal weight, only to discover that life was no different, you were still in the same job, the same house and the same relationship. Meanwhile you are bad-tempered, moody, irritable and your family suffer. Your emotions are ruled by what you eat. If you have had a 'good' eating day you are happy; if not, you are impossible.

ATTACK your problem. Accept that the quality of your life will not change whether you are a half-stone lighter or heavier.

GET your fears into perspective. You can travel on an aeroplane, nurse a sick mother, bring up children . . . but you cannot say 'No' to Auntie Maude's ginger cake?

STOP resenting the fact that you will have to cut out sweets and sugary 'treats'. The Eating Plan explains why it is vital not to eat these things in order to stabilise your blood sugar and get well again. You don't feel resentful or deprived when you face the choice between buying a new dress or a new pair of shoes; the same goes for your eating. You have the choice to be in control or out of control around food.

LEARN to accept the things you cannot change and change the things you can. You may have to change your lifestyle as well as your eating patterns. Start treating your mind instead of your stomach; give yourself positive distractions to food, go for a walk, take up a hobby, visit a friend. Just as compulsive eating has become a habit, so can writing letters, painting or making stained-glass windows. If it seems tough, work out how much time you waste thinking about food, feeling guilty about having a binge and the cost of your binges.

BELIEVE that you are loved for that sparkle in your eyes and your laughter, rather than the size of your waist.

CHALLENGE yourself to follow the Eating Plan. We are used to people complaining that it appears difficult to keep to it. This is because so many compulsive eaters have been on diets all their lives, and the only food they think of eating is cottage cheese and grapefruit. But this book shows that there is a great variety of foods that you can eat, that are healthy for your body, enjoyable and tasty to eat and which won't trigger a binge. Remember that most of the things worth achieving in life are not easy, whether it's passing exams, learning to drive or having a successful marriage. It must be more difficult to stay the way you are, living in the Food Trap, concealing your problem, lying about why the fridge is empty, why there is nothing for supper and where the housekeeping money has gone.

At times you will slip back . . . everyone does. You are not a failure if you learn by your mistakes. Listen to your mind and body, realise why you binged, what triggered it and what you should eat in the future to avoid it happening again. For instance, Claire slipped up because she weighed herself every day and when she put on a pound she felt so miserable she binged. We told her to throw her scales away and to stop being so obsessive. She learned from this mistake. If you are overweight, you will lose weight if you follow the Eating Plan, but it will not be overnight, so don't keep weighing yourself all the time. You will gradually get slimmer because you are eating fresh wholesome food and you will have stopped bingeing on high-calorie sugary processed products, cakes and biscuits. You will feel happier and look better too.

We know that the Eating Plan works if you have the right approach. Trust it and try it. It takes most people about one month to get their eating under control and after that you can experiment by trial and error to discover the foods you can add back to your diet which will not trigger a binge.

It is no good saying you cannot start the Eating Plan because of school holidays, Christmas is coming, the kitchen is being decorated, you are moving house or changing jobs. These things happen all the time and tomorrow there will be another excuse; but excuses won't cure you, stop making excuses and start the Eating Plan today.

2 The Eating Plan

There is no easy way out of the Food Trap. There are no magic pills or potions and conventional calorie-counting diets do not work, as anyone who has an eating problem will vouch.

Diets make you obsessive about food – you have to count calories, buy special food, weigh and measure each portion and you end up thinking about 'food' all the time. People who do not suffer from an eating problem are relaxed about food. One day they may be much hungrier than the next, but they don't feel guilty, they follow what their bodies tell them. Compulsive eaters have lost that ability. For many it starts when they begin to diet. They try to stick rigidly to 1,000 calories a day; they become hungry, binge, feel guilty and binge again. The downward spiral of feasting and fasting begins and you find yourself in the Eating Trap.

The Eating Plan is *not* a diet. It is *not* a temporary answer to your problem and there are *no* promises of fast instant weight loss. The plan has been devised to get your eating back to normal – permanently. By following the plan you will reach your goal weight, if it is reasonable, and stay there.

The plan suggests foods which will ensure you eat a healthy balanced diet. It explains which foods you can eat and why, and which foods should be avoided. At the Maisner Centre clients are given the Eating Plan, but we do not expect them to be able to stick to it immediately. We understand that if they could keep to a rigid diet, they would not have an eating problem anyway. We help them to solve their eating problem by studying where they went wrong. Clients are asked to fill in daily food charts, recording what they did eat, how hungry they were, where they ate and what mood they were in. (These charts are available from the Maisner Centre; see the address at the front of the book.) From the charts we can discover what triggers off a binge; it may be a certain time of day, mood or person; or they may be allergic to some food. This way we get to the root of the problem instead of forcing them to stick to an unnaturally strict diet.

There is one set of rules that you must follow, the Ten Commandments.

The Ten Commandments

1 Eat three meals and at least three snacks a day.
2 Start the day with a protein breakfast.
3 Eat sufficient protein every day (one gramme of protein per kilo of body weight).
4 Do not eat any refined foods.
5 Avoid concentrated sugars.
6 Do not eat breakfast cereals.
7 Do not drink alcohol.
8 Cut out caffeine from your diet.
9 Do not count calories.
10 Learn to relax and enjoy your food.

1 Eat three meals and at least three snacks a day

When you eat is as important as what you eat. Break away from the convention of eating three meals a day – if you are trying to stick rigidly to just three meals it is likely that you will feel hungry in between meals. Taking regular small meals is a vital step to getting your eating under control. This will stop you feeling too hungry, cut out the urge to binge and stop the guilt from eating in between meals.

Your body converts food into sugar and in turn into energy. If the level of sugar in the blood drops you feel tired, moody, depressed and hungry; just the right conditions to trigger a binge. If it continues to fall you begin to crave sweet things. The best way to maintain a constant blood sugar level is to eat frequent small protein-based meals and snacks. But you must eat good wholesome food and not sugary refined snacks or chocolate bars. A quick dose of refined sugar causes the blood sugar level to rise rapidly. This gives you a temporary lift but to compensate for this rush of unnatural sugar the body releases insulin, forcing the blood sugar level to plummet. This means you are back where you started, feeling tired and hungry. To keep the blood sugar level constant, eat protein foods with the addition of fruit and raw vegetables if you need a snack. The golden rule is *never to go longer than four hours without protein*.

2   *Start the day with a protein breakfast*

What you eat for breakfast affects how you feel for the rest of the day. If breakfast is nothing but coffee and a hurried bowl of sugary cereal, your blood sugar level will rocket and then fall rapidly by mid-morning, that's when you reach for a sticky bun or chocolate bar. The best sort of breakfast is a protein meal, such as chicken, ham or fish. You will be surprised how much energy you have the rest of the day if you try eating a nourishing breakfast.

3   *Eat sufficient protein every day*

Protein is vital building material, essential for the repair of body tissues. Any crash diet that doesn't include sufficient protein means you lose lean tissue and muscle and not fat, which leads to a rebound in weight gain and a flabby body.

Protein is digested slowly by the body; this means you will not find yourself feeling hungry and tired shortly after a meal. The best sources of protein are meat, fish, eggs, nuts, milk and soya products. It is also found in pulses, bread and potatoes, but these should not be eaten in large quantities until your eating is fully under control, particularly bread as this is a common trigger of binges for many compulsive eaters. The best sources of good quality protein are fish and poultry because these are low in fat and subsequently low in calories.

4   *Do not eat any refined foods*

The body's digestive system needs work to do if it is to remain healthy. Processed, refined and instant foods take all the work out of digestion, passing quickly through the system leaving you feeling hungry again shortly afterwards. It is vital to include some roughage in your diet every day. This can be found in vegetables, fruit and bran. Roughage will keep you feeling full longer than refined foods do and help prevent constipation, a common problem among those with eating problems. When your eating is under control and your diet includes bread, pasta and rice again, make sure you eat the wholegrain varieties, as these give fibre as well as extra vitamins and nutrients stripped away in the refining process.

5 Avoid concentrated sugars

The body only needs a small quantity of sugar and the only acceptable sugars are those found naturally and in diluted form, such as the lower calorie fruit and vegetables, and in milk. Refined sugar, whether brown or white, has been stripped of everything but calories. It is absorbed at a rapid rate and causes a dramatic temporary rise in the blood sugar level. Food packets may not list sugar in the ingredients but beware of food containing anything ending in 'ose', such as dextrose or fructose, because these are all sugars. It is better to try to lose your sweet-tooth, but if you really must sweeten your food use sugar substitutes. There are many products on the market that do not leave a bitter after-taste.

6 Do not eat breakfast cereals

Packets of breakfast cereals are now the traditional breakfast for many of us, but they almost all contain sugar and so are full of calories. As well as forcing the blood sugar level up, many people with eating disorders find that these cereals act as trigger foods, sending them on a binge. If you really must have a cereal breakfast, the lowest sugar content is found in Shredded Wheat (0.5 per cent) or porridge oats, which do contain protein, but they do not appear to satisfy compulsive eaters for as long as eating animal protein. Eat at least one-fifth of your daily protein intake at breakfast.

7 Do not drink alcohol

There are no exceptions to this rule while you are getting your eating under control; alcohol will lower your will-power and also your blood sugar level and lead to bingeing. It is also extremely fattening. If you have any difficulty giving up alcohol for a month, you may have a drink problem as well as an eating problem.

8 Cut out caffeine from your diet

Caffeine disturbs the blood sugar level and although drinking coffee may fulfil the appetite in the short term, over a longer period it will make you hungry. Caffeine also causes stress and anxiety, just the thing you don't need when you are trying to get your eating under control. If you are a heavy coffee drinker you should either go 'cold turkey' and cut it out completely, in which case it is possible you may feel a little ill for about four days; tiredness and headaches are common in these circumstances; or, better still, start cutting down gradually by blending your normal brand with decaffeinated coffee.

Tea also contains caffeine but weak tea is not too harmful, although you would be better to try and do without caffeine altogether. Herbal teas are useful provided you check the label to see if there is caffeine in them, but diet coke, except for Energen, is **OUT**!

9   Do not count calories

Traditional weight-reducing diets require you to count calories for each meal, every day. With the Eating Plan there are no calories to count because we believe that the more you worry about what you are eating, the bigger problem it causes you. People get very confused about calories. It is useful to have a broad idea of calorific values so you can avoid eating too much high calorie food which will make you put on weight.

10   Learn to relax and enjoy your food

Life does not exist around cottage cheese and grapefruit, counting calories and bathroom scales. The Eating Plan allows for plenty of variety, so start experimenting and don't be obsessed with what you eat. If you go out to dinner for a special occasion and are served a few chips or butter with your potatoes, eat them and enjoy it. It is not going to hurt just this once and you will only spoil the occasion by worrying. Unlike conventional diets we don't specify how much you should eat a day. This is because it is impossible to do that; what is suitable for a 78kg (12st) man who works on a building site is not the same for a 52kg (8st) female office worker. Also one day you may be hungrier than the next; there is a natural variation in appetite which has to be considered.

Initially if you stick to the Eating Plan, eat slowly and make the right food choices, you will lose weight. However, because the Eating Plan is an adjustment back to *normal* eating, you will lose weight slower than with a crash diet which produces a faster but only temporary weight loss. Don't weigh yourself for a month – the scales can sometimes be misleading. You can lose inches from around your waist before it starts to show on the scales. If you are not bingeing and not eating any high-calorie meals, it follows that you must be losing fat from your body.

Once your eating is under control, start listening to your body. Provided that you eat only when you are physically hungry, choose the right sorts of food and eat slowly, you will continue to lose weight if you need to. The Eating Plan ensures that by eating many small meals and snacks you never get too hungry, because this leads to bingeing and bad food choices.

The Eating Plan is a general guide to choosing the foods each day which will put your eating back on the right path. You do not need to follow the examples, instead make your own choices and try as many alternatives as possible. In fact, you can eat whatever you like as long as it follows the rules of the Ten Commandments. Use your imagination to give your meals plenty of variety so you do not get bored. For instance, the first column is an example of a day's eating. But if you do not like eggs, a suitable breakfast alternative to egg and bacon might be a slice of low-fat cheese and tomato, or half a tin of tuna in brine mixed with half a carton of cottage cheese.

We have not put the times of the day you should eat the meals as your mealtimes will vary according to your lifestyle. For example, if you have a late breakfast and an early lunch you may need two afternoon snacks, or if you have a late lunch and an early supper you may need two evening snacks. The principle of the Eating Plan always remains the same, and remember, NEVER go more than four hours without a protein snack.

The Eating Plan is a general guide – you should make your own choice and have as much variety as possible. We have not put the times for meals as they could vary according to your lifestyle. If you have a late breakfast and an early lunch you may need two afternoon snacks and if you have a late lunch and early supper you may need two evening snacks. The principle remains the same and NEVER go more than 4 hours without a snack.

The Eating Plan

	Example of a day's eating	Example of a day's eating for a VEGETARIAN
ON RISING	Citrus fruit – if allergic choice from Box II	Orange juice
BREAKFAST	Box I – compulsory Boxes II, III, VII – optional *All other Boxes optional**	Boiled egg and Ryvita	Natural yogurt with sunflower and sesame seeds
MID-MORNING SNACK	Box I – compulsory Boxes II or III and VII – optional *All other Boxes optional**	Yogurt and apple	Celery and tahini dip
LUNCHTIME	Box I – compulsory Boxes II, III, VI, VII – optional *All other Boxes optional**	Tinned tuna fish in brine with coleslaw and beetroot	Cheese on toast with a mixed salad
MID-AFTERNOON SNACK	Box I – compulsory Boxes II or III and VII – optional *All other Boxes optional**	Cod's roe on lettuce with cucumber	Cottage cheese and fresh fruit
SUPPER	Box I – compulsory Boxes II, III, VI, VII – optional *All other Boxes optional**	(a) Home-made soup (if required) (b) Chicken, broccoli heads and mixed salad (c) Choice from Box VI if required	(a) Lentil and vegetable soup (b) Mushroom omelette, spinach, dash of soya sauce (c) Choice from Box VI if required
MID-EVENING AND/ OR BEDTIME	Choice of Boxes I, II or III	Cottage Cheese and an apple	Skimmed milk drink with vanilla essence

* Italic choices are for those people who want to gain weight or who are at the right weight and are in control of their eating.

Note 1 Crispbreads and wholemeal bread can be eaten, but if you have a weight problem you obviously will only eat small amounts. You should try to vary the types of bread, such as rye, corn and pumpernickel. Bran added to soups, yogurts, etc. make a useful low-calorie filler.

Note 2 IF YOU ARE FOLLOWING A DIET PRESCRIBED BY YOUR DOCTOR FOR SPECIFIC MEDICAL REASONS OTHER THAN EATING PROBLEMS YOU SHOULD CONSULT WITH HIM BEFORE EMBARKING ON THIS EATING PLAN. IF YOU KNOW OF ANY FOODS THAT CAUSE MEDICAL PROBLEMS OR HAVE ANY KNOWN FOOD ALLERGIES, AVOID THESE FOODS – THERE ARE ALWAYS ALTERNATIVES

Table 2.1

BOX I PROTEIN FOODS

Eggs
Unprocessed fresh meat
Poultry
Fish (fresh and tinned in brine)
Offal
Dairy products
Soya products, ie Tofu, TVP
Nuts
Pulses

BOX II FRUIT

All fresh fruits, except bananas.
Grapes should be eaten with caution.
Absolutely no dried fruit.
Tinned fruit which is packed in
water or prepared especially for
diabetics is suitable. Always read
the labels.

BOX III VEGETABLES

All fresh and frozen vegetables are
permissible.
Potatoes should be boiled in their
skins or baked in their jackets.
Tinned vegetables, if they are not
packed with sugar, are also
suitable.

BOX IV CARBOHYDRATES

1 Wholemeal bread, crispbreads
and bran can be added to any of
your meals, provided you do
not have any problems with
them. If they prove to be a
trigger food, they should be
avoided for the time being. You
should try to vary the types of
bread you eat, such as rye or
corn and pumpernickel.

2 Brown rice, porridge oats,
Shredded Wheat are fairly high
in calories and should be eaten
only in moderation if you have a
weight problem.

3 *The foods listed below are
completely forbidden:*

Sugar, jams, molasses, honey,
marmalade, syrups, white flour,
pasta, rice. Soft drinks which
contain sugar, cakes, biscuits,
manufactured ice creams.

BOX V EXTRAS

The foods listed below will not
affect your blood sugar level. They
are all permissible but are all very
high calorie, and should not be
eaten excessively if you wish to
lose weight.

Fats, oils, butter and margarine,
mayonnaise and salad dressings (if
shop-bought, watch the labels for
sugar), avocados.

BOX VI DESSERTS

Junket (home-made)
Fresh fruit
Tinned fruit packed in water
Cheeses
Home-made jellies and mousses
Diet Ski and Shape fruit yogurts
Natural sugar-free yogurts

BOX VII BEVERAGES

Water, soda and Perrier
Herb teas
Unsweetened fresh fruit juices
Milk
Consommé
Bovril
Decaffeinated coffee

Make use of as many of the alternatives as possible; in fact you can eat whatever you like as long as it follows the Ten Commandments. Use your imagination to give your diet plenty of variety so you don't get bored; for example, if you don't like eggs, a suitable breakfast alternative for egg and bacon, might be slice of low fat cheese and tomato, or half a tin of tuna in brine mixed with half a carton of cottage cheese.

Protein Value of Foods in Relation to Calories

The following tables will help you to make the best choices when it comes to selecting the foods which are low in calories and high in protein. For example, if you wish to eat cheese you will see from the chart that while Cheddar may have twice as much protein as cottage cheese, it has four times as many calories. We do not want you to become obsessive about counting calories but it is better to have an idea of the calorie-content of food to ensure you are eating sufficient protein without too many calories.

A more complete list of foods with their protein and calorie content is available in McCance and Widdowson's *The Composition of Foods* (HMSO).

Amounts of protein in different foods

Meat	Calories per 100g (3½ oz)	Protein per 100g (3½ oz)
BACON		
lean, raw	147	20.2
gammon rashers, lean, grilled	172	31.4
middle rashers, lean and fat, grilled	416	24.1
BEEF		
lean, average, raw	123	20.3
brisket, boiled, lean and fat	326	27.6
mince, stewed	229	23.1
stewing steak, stewed, lean and fat	223	30.9
topside roast, lean and fat	214	26.6

	Calories per 100g (3½ oz)	Protein per 100g (3½ oz)
LAMB		
lean, average, raw	162	20.8
chops, lean and fat, grilled	355	23.5
leg, roast, lean and fat	266	26.1
breast, roast, lean only	252	25.6
shoulder, roast, lean and fat	316	19.9
PORK		
lean, average, raw	147	20.7
chops, grilled, lean & fat	332	28.5
leg, roast, lean only	185	30.7
VEAL		
fillet, raw	109	21.1
roast	230	31.6
CHICKEN (Turkey slightly less on calories and protein)		
raw, meat only	121	20.5
boiled meat only	183	29.2
roast, meat only	148	24.8
leg, quarter (weighed with bone)	92	15.4
OFFAL		
heart, stewed (ox)	179	31.4
kidney, stewed (pig)	153	24.4
kidney, lamb, raw	90	16.5
liver, lamb, raw	179	20.1
liver, ox, stewed	198	24.8
oxtail, stewed	243	30.5

Fish

	Calories per 100g (3½ oz)	Protein per 100g (3½ oz)
COD		
grilled	95	20.8
poached	94	20.9
HADDOCK		
steamed	98	22.8
smoked, steamed	101	23.3
HERRING		
grilled	199	20.4

	Calories per 100g (3½ oz)	Protein per 100g (3½ oz)
SARDINES		
in oil	289	22.8
TUNA		
in oil	289	22.8
TROUT		
brown, steamed	135	23.5
SHELLFISH		
crab, boiled	127	20.1
prawns, boiled	107	22.6
mussels, boiled	87	17.2

Non-animal protein food

Soya bean pâté	132	10.8
T.V.P. Beef flavour	250	51.5
Sweet and sour flavour	250	51.5
Chicken flavour	227	46.0
Bologna	167	20.1
Sausalatas	137	11.0
Nut brawn	212	8.3
Dinner balls	225	14.0
Liquid soya milk	51	3.6
Soya flour, full fat	447	36.8
Soya flour, low fat	352	45.3

Milk and milk products

MILK (COWS')		
fresh, whole	65	3.3
fresh, skimmed	33	3.4
BUTTER		
salted	740	0.4
CREAM		
single	212	2.4
double	447	1.5
whipping	332	1.9
CHEESE		
Camembert type	300	22.8

	Calories per 100g (3½ oz)	Protein per 100g (3½ oz)
Cheddar type	406	26.0
Edam type	304	24.4
Cottage cheese	96	13.6
Cheese spread	183	18.3
YOGURT (low fat)		
Natural	52	5.0
EGGS		
whole, raw	147	12.3

Cereals

BREAD		
wholemeal	216	8.8
brown	223	8.9
BREAKFAST CEREAL		
Shredded Wheat	324	10.6
Cooked porridge	44	1.4

Vegetables

green mung beans, raw	231	22.0
red kidney beans, boiled	87	22.1
butter beans, boiled	95	7.1
haricot beans, boiled	93	6.6
lentils, split, boiled	99	7.6
peas, fresh boiled	52	5.0
peas, dried raw	286	21.6
sweetcorn, boiled	123	4.1
potatoes (old), boiled	80	1.4
potatoes (old), baked	85	2.1

Fruit

Avocado pears	223	4.2

Nuts

Almonds	565	16.9
Brazils	619	12.0
Chestnuts	170	2.0

	Calories per 100g (3½ oz)	Protein per 100g (3½ oz)
Hazels	380	7.6
Peanuts	570	24.3
Peanut butter	623	22.6
Walnuts	525	10.6

3 'It's bad for me.'

Compulsive eaters often say they cannot follow the Eating Plan because 'I cannot eat this,' or 'I cannot eat that.' They claim that certain foods in the plan are 'bad' for them, yet conveniently forget that bingeing is far worse for their health. Most compulsive eaters are not so fussy when it comes to the food they binge on – puddings, biscuits, cakes and pies.

If you eat vast quantities of any one food, whether it is bread, fruit or cream, it will be bad for you. Our aim is to teach moderation and, hopefully, end your obsession with food. Try to put what you eat into perspective. I was spotted by a client eating a hamburger and wholemeal roll; she told me: 'That's bad for you.' In fact, it was the first time for five years I had eaten a hamburger and, as I was tired and hungry and at a railway station, a hamburger was the best choice I could make from the Buffet Bar. It did no harm to eat it, not only did the hamburger contain protein and the roll provide fibre, but I needed to eat at that time and it was better for me than a chocolate bar.

By following the Eating Plan you will begin to understand the effect that food has on you, and then you can work out for yourself which foods are bad for you.

'Too much protein is bad for you.'

Too much of anything can be bad for you. If you eat nothing but vast amounts of protein, your health will suffer, but the Eating Plan does not suggest you eat an unhealthy amount. Modern thinking about diet and health recommends eating less protein than we have in the past. But the eating needs of compulsive eaters are different from those who do not suffer from an eating problem. Nutritionists may recommend less eggs and red meat and plenty of brown rice, brown bread and pulses instead, but these do not sustain a compulsive eater's appetite for as long as animal protein. They also contain poorer quality protein and they are higher in calories, as you can see in Table 3.1.

Table 3.1   Protein – amounts needed and Calorie value

	Cals per 100g (3½ oz)	Protein per 100g (3½ oz)	Cals for 10g (¼ oz) protein	Amount for 10g (¼ oz) protein
Gelatine*	338	84.4	40	12g (½ oz)
Egg white	36	9.0	40	111g (4 oz)
Marmite	179	41.4	43	24g (1 oz)
Cod	76	17.4	44	57g (2 oz)
Sainsbury's skim milk cheese (Quark)	80	16.5	48	61g (2 oz)
Shrimps, shelled and boiled	117	23.8	49	42g (1½ oz)
Kidney, no core	90	16.5	55	61g (2 oz)
Chicken, no skin or fat	121	20.5	59	49g (1¾ oz)
Mushrooms	13	1.8	72	556g (19½ oz)
Tendale cheese	253	29.5	86	34g (1¼ oz)
Skim milk, dry	355	36.4	98	27g (1 oz)
Eggs (whole)	147	12.3	120	81g (2¾ oz)
Soya beans/flour	447	36.8	121	27g (1 oz)
Lentils, boiled	99	7.6	130	132g (4½ oz)
Peanuts	570	24.3	235	41g (1½ oz)
Brown bread	223	8.9	251	112g (4 oz)
Spaghetti, boiled	117	4.2	279	238g (8½ oz)
Potatoes, boiled	80	1.4	571	714g (25 oz)

Best quality protein: Eggs, biological value of 100 which means it is absorbed 100 per cent into the human body.

Good quality protein: Milk, cheese, fish, meat, soya BV 70 (70 per cent only absorbed)

Poor quality protein: Bread, cereals, nuts (50 per cent or less absorbed)

Poor quality protein: Gelatine*

* Lacks tryptophan – an essential amino acid – so should be used with milk or eggs.

We have helped many thousands of compulsive eaters at the Maisner Centre and have found they all do better if they eat some animal protein. Once they have controlled their eating habits, compulsive eaters can adjust their eating to bring it in line with what they consider to be a healthy diet.

I believe you are better off eating so-called 'bad' food, such as eggs and cheese, and getting your eating under control, rather than bingeing on chocolate bars and tins of custard because your protein intake is too low.

'I cannot eat cream because it's fattening.'

Cream is included in the Eating Plan because it does not affect your blood sugar, but it is fattening if you eat it regularly. Many compulsive eaters do not have a weight problem; often they are underweight, so it would not harm them to eat cream occasionally. Remember that this is not a typical weight-loss diet anyway, and it is far better for you to have an occasional bowl of strawberries with a dollop of cream than to binge on packets of biscuits. If you don't want to eat cream, simply do not use the recipes which include it. In many cases you could substitute yogurt for cream.

'Butter is bad for you.'

Butter will not affect your blood sugar, but it is fattening if used in any quantity. If you don't want to eat butter, then use polyunsaturated margarine instead. The recipes in this book do include some fat but you can exclude the fat from many of them or use a smaller quantity if you wish to. Remember also, soups and stews can be cooked and placed in the fridge overnight, allowing the fat to harden so it can be skimmed off before reheating.

'I have got high blood pressure and my doctor says I cannot eat meat.'

You do not have to eat meat; there are many other sources of protein included in the Eating Plan, such as fish and poultry. Large binges will have a far greater effect on your blood pressure than eating a steak occasionally.

'My doctor says I must not eat . . .'

There is no need to eat food forbidden by your doctor. Simply leave it out of your diet and choose some other food – there is plenty of choice in the Eating Plan.

'Eating bran deprives you of iron.'

Bran does provide essential fibre which prevents constipation, a common problem among compulsive eaters. It is far better to lose a little iron than to take twenty laxatives. You will lose far more minerals and vitamins through purging than eating bran a few times a week. If you do not like wheat bran you could always use soya or oat bran. Oat bran is particularly good used as a thickener in casseroles and soups, or why not make sure you get sufficient fibre from other sources such as fruit, vegetables and unrefined carbohydrates.

'Food with additives is bad for you.'

Unfortunately, almost everything we eat contains additives, even the more natural products, such as yogurt, cottage cheese and fruit-flavoured drinks. The only way to avoid additives completely is to go back to the land, keep a goat and chickens and grow your own vegetables. However, you will still be in the Food Trap, obsessed about your food. Keeping off sugar and refined carbohydrates and making sure you do eat a balanced diet with lots of fresh fruit and vegetables as well as meat, chicken and fish, will compensate for the few additives you do consume following the Eating Plan.

4 'I don't like breakfast.'

Breakfast is the most important meal of the day. What you eat first thing in the morning affects how you feel for the rest of the day, dictating whether you will be bright and lively, or sluggish and irritable.

During the night your blood sugar level drops and this can make you feel moody and bad-tempered when you wake up. Most household arguments start before or during breakfast and research shows that many industrial accidents are caused by workers who have not eaten breakfast. Children who skip breakfast do not do as well at school because they find it difficult to concentrate.

In the past breakfast was recognised as the most important meal of the day. In the eighteenth and nineteenth centuries the great British breakfast reached its height with numerous courses including everything from game pies, chops, kedgeree, fish, mutton and beef as well as eggs and toast with preserves.

Not so long ago breakfast was still considered an important family occasion. Mums and dads and the children would sit down together to discuss the day ahead over their eggs and bacon. These days such a picture is becoming rarer as busy mums hand out cups of coffee and bowls of cereal and would not consider cooking a proper meal.

Coffee and cereal may be convenient, but they don't do you any good. Sugar-coated cereals create a rapid rise in your blood sugar level, but the body releases insulin to compensate and the blood sugar plummets – that is why you find yourself reaching for a mid-morning pastry or chocolate bar. Coffee does not supply you with any nourishment, and the caffeine it contains disturbs the blood sugar level, leaving you feeling tired and hungry.

Traditional breakfasts, such as bacon and eggs, are given the cold-shoulder by many who think such a meal is fattening and too heavy first thing in the morning. Yet such breakfasts are full of protein and constitute the best way to start the day. You do not have to have eggs and bacon; try slices of beef, chicken livers on wholemeal toast, cottage cheese with chopped fruit, yogurt with pumpkin and sesame seeds, palma ham and melon, or even salmon. Breakfast can be dull or exciting, cheap or as expensive as you like, but the important thing to remember is to try to consume at least one-fifth of your daily intake of protein at this meal.

Compulsive eaters who do not eat breakfast are almost guaranteed to binge at the end of the day. You have nothing to lose by trying to eat breakfast: you will not need that mid-morning pastry, you will not feel tired and moody by lunchtime and you should not binge either. Instead, you will be full of energy and much happier.

'I have not got the time.'

Get up 10 minutes earlier. Breakfast is a vital step to getting your eating under control. You can always find time to do the things you really want to in the mornings, like cleaning your teeth, going to the toilet, getting dressed, brushing your hair and probably putting on some make-up. So start finding time for breakfast. It does not take long to eat something nourishing, like opening a tub of cottage cheese or taking a slice of ham out of the packet.

'I cannot face breakfast.'

This is usually a sign of low blood sugar. If you eat a poor breakfast or none at all your blood sugar level will drop even lower and by mid-morning you will be craving a sugary snack.

No desire for breakfast can also be a sign of eating too much the night before. For most people the evening meal is the main meal of the day, but if you eat a plate piled with stodgy food and then nibble at biscuits and cakes for the rest of the evening while sitting in front of the television, the food will not be properly digested. This means that in the morning you have little appetite. Change your eating habits. It is much more sensible to start the day with a proper balanced meal to give you the energy for the rest of the day and to eat a lighter meal in the evening. Your body becomes accustomed to eating times – and bad habits. You are prepared to take medicines and pills to remedy illness, you must be prepared to take some action to solve your eating problem and make yourself well again. It may be tough getting used to having breakfast, but after following the Eating Plan for a while you will begin to feel hungry in the mornings. In the meantime force yourself to take something at breakfast, even if you can only manage a glass of milk.

'I don't like breakfast.'

That is probably why you have an eating problem. Ask yourself if you dislike breakfast more than you hate bingeing. Habits can be broken. Start telling yourself that you DO like breakfast, and you WILL. Think positively each morning when you get up that you will eat some breakfast. You can choose from such a wide variety of foods that contain protein, including meat, poultry, fish, dairy products, beans and pulses. There must be some food that you like from the list that you could eat for breakfast.

'I don't like eggs for breakfast.'

Fried, boiled or scrambled, eggs are the traditional British breakfast, but that does not mean that you have to eat them. You don't have to stick to packets of breakfast cereal either. Start the day by eating something that you do like that contains sufficient protein: you have plenty of choice.

'Too many eggs are bad for you.'

It is true that eggs contain cholesterol which, in large quantities, can clog up the arteries in some people, but there is no doubt that binges of chocolate and bread and butter sandwiches in large quantities do even more damage! There is also an old wives' tale that says eggs cause constipation. This is true when protein-only diets are followed, but eggs eaten with sufficient roughage do not cause constipation. However, there is *no need* to eat eggs for breakfast, yet it is better to have an egg each morning than to binge all day. It is a question of balancing your diet and if you follow the Eating Plan you will be consuming enough roughage to ensure you do not suffer from constipation, even if you eat eggs each day. Belinda stopped bingeing and vomiting after she began to eat a boiled egg for breakfast. The egg contained protein which stabilised her blood sugar level and started the day in a healthy way. Then she began to worry that she would have a heart attack because she was eating too many eggs. She stopped eating eggs and would not eat any other form of protein for breakfast, and she started to binge again.

Eggs alone will not cause a heart attack. Carry on eating eggs and get your fears into proportion. Anything must be better than a binge, even eating eggs, but why not choose another form of protein if you are unhappy about eggs?

If your doctor has put you on a low-cholesterol diet, you should not eat more than two eggs a week. But check why your cholesterol level is high, it could be because of your bingeing.

'If I eat breakfast I never stop eating all day.'

Are you eating because you are hungry, or for some other reason, loneliness, frustration or boredom? If you are not making excuses and you do genuinely feel hungry, then it is probably due to a certain food rather than breakfast itself. Many compulsive eaters find that binges are triggered by a certain food, and breakfast cereals are a common cause. Even if breakfast cereals do not trigger a binge, they still affect your blood sugar level. After causing an initial lift, your blood sugar level will rapidly drop and you will feel tired, hungry and may start craving sweet things. If you succumb to temptation the same circle will repeat itself and you will be eating a lot all day, but quickly feeling hungry again.

Jane complained that when she ate breakfast she could not stop eating all day. Yet her 'healthy' breakfast was a sugary cereal followed by toast and marmalade, with the result that her blood sugar level dropped and by mid-morning she was tucking into a Danish pastry. A few hours later, she felt tired and hungry again for something sweet. She went through this routine all day. Then she started to eat protein for breakfast, such as ham on a piece of wholemeal toast, yogurt or cottage cheese with nuts or fruit, and from the first day, she noticed the difference. She no longer felt the need to eat something sweet mid-morning and she had more energy to last her right up until her next snack.

One tip – after breakfast clean your teeth to take away the taste of the food: the 'hangover' taste of food often keeps you eating after a meal, even though you are no longer feeling at all hungry. Besides being a healthy habit, it will take you out of the kitchen and food never tastes so good once you have brushed your teeth.

Some ideas for healthy, protein breakfasts

1 *Egg and fruit whip* – simply beat a raw egg into a quarter of a pint of fruit juice.

2 *Yogurt and sesame seeds* – this has a wonderful laxative effect.

3 *Sugar-free baked beans.*

4 *Cottage cheese* – either on its own or with crispbreads or fruit, or tinned fish such as tuna in brine.

5 *Yogurt* – either on its own or with pumpkin seeds, fresh or stewed fruit.

6 *Eggs* – in any shape or form.

7 *Cold meats* – such as poultry, ham or beef.

8 *Porridge* – made of rolled oats with skimmed milk, either on its own or with fresh or stewed fruits or nuts.

9 *Skimmed milk* – either on its own in a glass or flavoured with decaffeinated coffee or with fruit whipped up in it.

10 *Herring roes on wholemeal toast.*

11 *Grilled herrings, kippers or smoked haddock.*

12 *Breakfast kedgeree* – see following recipe.

13 *Scrambled kidneys (special)* – see following recipe.

14 *Egg ramekins* – see following recipe.

15 *Cheese* – either on its own or on wholemeal toast.

16 *Bacon* – grilled with mushrooms or tomatoes.

BREAKFAST KEDGEREE
450g (1lb) smoked haddock
Bay leaf
225g (8oz) brown rice
50g (2oz) button mushrooms, chopped
2 eggs, hard-boiled
2 tbsp skimmed milk
Freshly ground pepper
2 tbsp chopped parsley (optional)

Serves 4

Place the haddock in a pan with enough cold water to just cover and poach over a low heat for 10-12 minutes until soft but still firm. Take the fish out of the pan. Place the juices in a jug and make up to 500ml (18fl oz) with cold water, then pour into a pan, add the bay leaf, rice and chopped mushrooms and bring to the boil. Lower heat and simmer gently for about 40 minutes, until most of the stock has been absorbed, and the rice is just soft.

Flake the cooked fish and chop the hard-boiled eggs. Add these to the rice together with the skimmed milk. Heat until the milk is absorbed. Add pepper to taste.

Garnish with parsley and serve immediately.

SCRAMBLED KIDNEYS
50g (2oz) butter
225g (8oz) lambs' kidneys, skinned, cored and chopped
100g (4oz) mushrooms, sliced
1 tbsp chopped parsley
8 eggs
Salt and pepper
2 tbsp milk

Serves 4

Place 25g (1oz) of the butter in a saucepan, add the kidneys and sauté for 5 minutes. Then add the mushrooms and parsley and cook for a further 2 minutes. Place on one side and keep warm.

Beat together the eggs, salt and pepper. Melt the remaining butter in a saucepan, add the eggs and cook over a low heat, stirring continuously until the eggs are just setting. Remove from the heat and stir in the milk.

Place the scrambled eggs on a serving dish and pour the kidney mixture over the top. Serve with wholemeal toast.

EGG RAMEKINS
100g (4oz) low fat spread
4 tomatoes, skinned and chopped
Salt and pepper
2 tbsp chives, chopped
4 eggs

50g (2oz) ham (optional)
Chopped parsley for garnish (optional)

Serves 4

Pre-heat the oven to 425°F/220°C, gas mark 7. Grease four ramekin dishes with some of the low fat spread, then divide the chopped tomatoes equally between the four dishes, add the seasoning and the chives, and the ham if used. Break one egg into each dish and top with a scoop of the low fat spread. Bake in the oven until the eggs have set.

Garnish with chopped parsley and serve immediately.

APPLE PORRIDGE
250ml (8fl oz) skimmed milk
40g (1½oz) rolled oats
100g (4oz) stewed apple
½ tsp powdered cinnamon
3 drops vanilla essence
½ tsp artificial sweetener

Serves 2

Heat the milk until just boiling, then add the oats and stir until thickened. Add the stewed apple, cinnamon, vanilla and sweetener.

5 'I'm hard up.'

You should not need to make lack of money an excuse for being unable to keep to the Eating Plan. The plan includes fresh, nutritious food which is, on the whole, much cheaper than processed manufactured products. If you think you are short of money as a consequence of following the Eating Plan take a careful look at what you are really spending your money on – bottles of wine, perhaps, or new clothes? Surely your health should take priority over any other spending? Work out whether the cost of keeping to the plan and getting well again is worth the effort of cutting back in other areas of your life.

Ironically, the history of the twentieth century shows that during times of hardship people tend to eat a healthier diet than in times of ease and plenty. During the Second World War, at the peak of food rationing, the total allowance of sugar and fat for each adult every week was 225g (8oz). Think how much of that allowance would be used up in just a few of those treats you allow yourself, like a couple of doughnuts, a slice of toast dripping with butter and a fruit pie. Yet because of such rationing it is now generally believed that people were much healthier.

Today we are fortunate to live in an affluent country where almost everyone can afford to buy more than the basic essentials to maintain life. This has meant that nearly everybody eats too much, especially too much of the wrong food, and as a nation our health has suffered. So if money is short and it is difficult to make ends meet, what a splendid opportunity to cut out all those unnecessary extras. Spend what little money you have wisely on food and cut out the 'empty' calories, those foods that are often expensive but offer little in the way of nutrition. Don't feel deprived because you cannot afford to buy a fancy box of chocolates; you know you should not be buying things like that anyway if you have an eating problem and are following the Eating Plan.

'I cannot afford to buy nutritious food.'

Tracey claimed she could only afford to buy fish fingers and other processed food for herself and her children. She thought that packaged meals worked out cheaper than fresh ones. Packed, processed and manufactured goods cost *much* more than their fresh equivalents; after all someone has to pay for all the labour and machinery involved in turning out ready-made, frozen, brightly packaged meals.

Preparing your own meals from fresh ingredients may take a little longer, but it will not only be much cheaper, but more nutritious too. For example, a ready-made meal of frozen minced beef in gravy with vegetables can be priced at around 72p. It contains approximately 75g (3oz) of mince and 75g (3oz) of vegetables, while a trip to the butcher and the greengrocer could provide the same amount of meat and vegetables for not more than 30p. Just put them in a saucepan and simmer and you have something just as good, much cheaper, and with no dubious colourings and preservatives. (Later in this chapter there are suggestions showing how to survive the Eating Plan on a rock-bottom income.)

'I always spend too much money at the supermarket.'

One of the best tips for sensible shopping is to make a shopping list before you go out and to stick to it rigidly once you get to the shops. Work out exactly what you need and what you can afford to buy, and write out your list at a time when you are feeling in control. After a meal is a better time to think about shopping than when you are hungry. Never be tempted by colourful displays in the supermarket, they are cleverly designed to make you part with your money. Supermarkets invest large sums in working out devious ways of getting you to spend more than you intended – that is how they stay in business. So if you are short of money, don't fall for their alluring tricks. No matter how tempting, if it isn't on your list, don't buy it. You don't need it and you can't afford it.

'It's cheaper to buy in bulk, but then I over-eat.'

Most goods are cheaper if you buy in bulk, especially if you go direct to a wholesale market. Fruit and vegetables are a good example; for instance, while the wholesale price for 123 Jaffa oranges was £5.60 (4½p each), the greengrocer's price was 18p for a similar fruit. The wholesale market price for 14 melons was £7, while the greengrocer charged £1.50 each. The same applies to meat and fish; for example, wholesale cod at £12 for 6½kg (14lb), compared to the shop price of £1.99 for 450g (1lb).

If you find the idea of 123 Jaffas a bit daunting, think about getting together with a few friends or neighbours, and taking it in turns to go bulk shopping and dividing the foods between you. It is also important to find a good local wholesaler, you won't be saving any money if you have to lose a day's wages and drive a hundred miles to Covent Garden just to buy a crate of apples. If you want to go into bulk buying in a serious way it is well worth investing in a freezer. Sensible use of a deep freeze can save a small fortune, whether you have a large family or live alone.

If you are feeling more than usually hard up, this is not the time to suggest splashing out on a freezer and mountains of cod, but it is the right time to take a serious look at the long-term savings. Perhaps next time you have a little spare cash you could put it towards a freezer, or start trying to save a little each week with the aim of buying one in a year or so.

It is safe, and economical, to buy food like fish and cabbage in bulk, but don't allow large amounts of your favourite binge foods to lurk around the house. If you have litres of ice cream in the freezer, you know you will end up eating most of it yourself. It may seem clever to buy a bargain pack of cheese, instead of a small slice, but it is a false economy if you end up eating the whole lot.

'I cannot resist the special offers.'

If you spot something that you would normally buy at full price being offered at a cheaper price, it is worth stocking up, *provided* it is something that can be stored and will not tempt you to binge. It is useless buying three times as much and then eating it all at once. If you are disciplining your shopping by sticking to a list, remember that supermarket offers usually last more than one day. Make a mental note of a special offer and when you come to write your next shopping list, consider whether it is worth buying it; if so put it on your list; if not don't write it down and don't change your mind and buy it anyway when you get to the shop. The best offers to watch out for are seasonal. Buy your turkey in August, as the price shoots up just before Christmas, and buy vegetables and fruit when they are at their most plentiful and cheapest and freeze them.

'Vegetables are so expensive.'

The cost of fresh vegetables must work out cheaper than the cost of bingeing on cakes and biscuits, and be much better for you. If you have a garden, grow your own vegetables and fruit – you will get plenty of fresh air and exercise at the same time. Picking your own vegetables from farms will save you money and is becoming increasingly popular, but don't be in too much of a hurry to get picking as prices usually drop as each item reaches its peak.

'Proper lunches work out too expensive.'

Paula spent at least a pound a day on a take-away hamburger or chicken and chips because, she said, she could not afford a proper meal each day. True, it takes time and effort to make your own lunch, but it can work out much cheaper and will almost certainly be more nutritious. Try putting aside one evening a week to prepare home-made meals for the coming week. Choose simple recipes that will keep in the fridge and that can be carried easily. For example, you could make a bowl of your own coleslaw which will keep in the refrigerator for several days. Roast a chicken and divide it up so you have a portion of cooked chicken to take to the office for your lunch each day; it is much cheaper than buying a ready-cooked chicken quarter each lunchtime. A prawn sandwich might cost you 93p ready-made in a shop, but you could buy a packet of prawns for a similar amount that would last for several days' worth of sandwiches. If you like to eat a yogurt with your lunch every day, making your own can work out at around half the price of buying commercially made ones, and you can be sure there are no colourings and preservatives in it.

Free foods

Don't forget food you can get for free, like dandelion leaves that make an excellent alternative to lettuce in the spring, or even dandelion roots, which when scrubbed, dried and roasted, can be ground to make a caffeine-free 'coffee'. There are a number of useful books available that are full of ideas for food you can forage for yourself from the hedgerows. Do make sure you know exactly what you are picking, however, particularly when it comes to mushrooms.

And of course don't forget that wonderful drink that is always on tap; a glass of water is just as refreshing as costly cans of 'diet' fizzy drinks, and much better for you as well.

Get sprouting

The Chinese have known about the nutritional and economical benefits of sprouting seeds and beans for a long time. From a few tiny seeds you can grow a vast amount of sprouts for salads, sandwiches and main meals. All you need for sprouting is a glass jar and a piece of muslin held in place over the mouth of the jar by an elastic band. Soak the seeds overnight in water, drain, wash in fresh water and drain again so no water remains in the jar. Lay the jar of seeds on its side with the muslin cover in place, put it somewhere out of direct sunlight but where it is warm and there is plenty of ventilation. Every morning and evening remove the muslin cover and rinse and drain the seeds. In a few days you will have a good crop of vitamin-packed sprouts.

Saving fuel

Invest in a pressure cooker, a slow cooker or a microwave; providing you make good use of them they will soon pay for themselves with the savings you will make on fuel. You will be able to prepare an excellent meal in a short space of time with a pressure cooker, and although you need to get up a few minutes earlier in the morning to prepare the meal and switch on a slow cooker, when you get home at night your meal is ready and you can eat straight away without being tempted to nibble while you are cooking. Careful use of a microwave saves both time and money.

The real secret of how to save money on food is good planning. Think ahead about your shopping and cooking and plan the most economical ways of catering. You will soon find your efficiency pays off.

If you always seem to be hard up, take a close look at your lifestyle. Perhaps you really are on a low income, maybe you could consider changing your job or getting a second job part-time, selling party plan or working at home. Not only would this bring in more money but it will leave you with less time for unplanned snacks. If you are already working as many hours as you feel you can, you should be earning enough to buy suitable food to follow the Eating Plan.

Ask yourself if you are spending too much money on other areas of your life: is the mortgage too big, do you really need an expensive foreign holiday this summer, or can you make do with last year's winter coat instead of buying a new one? It is up to you to decide how you spend your money, but surely getting your eating under control and being well again should be top of your list of priorities. Perhaps you will solve your money problems when you solve your eating problem; have you just been spending too much money on binges?

HINTS ON HOW TO COPE WITH THE
EATING PLAN ON A VERY, VERY LOW BUDGET

The National Average of expenditure on food *in the home* as part of the housewife's budget is just over £8 (1985) per week. Money spent on snacks, restaurants, canteens, chocolate, alcohol, etc. is additional, so for many the total food cost is much higher. The average includes children, so if only adults are concerned the figure will be higher still – probably £10.00 and over. In planning an economy diet for an adult it is desirable to aim to keep under £5.00 per week – 71p per day – to allow for optional extras.

LUXURIES to be included will be anything which does not provide essential nutrients – though the luxury of flavour or convenience can be added to the diet whenever extra money becomes available. Even the poorest races like to save up for a feast on special occasions! THE THREE CRITICAL FACTORS ARE PROTEIN, MICRO–NUTRIENTS AND CALORIES –

PROTEIN is always relatively expensive so must be planned first. CALORIES are included up to the level of 1,500 to 2,000 per day at no extra expense, but will increase the total cost considerably when heavy manual work requires 2,500 and over. MICRO-NUTRIENTS – the combined term for VITAMINS and ESSENTIAL MINERALS – determine the choices to be made, and involve the most work in planning a diet – and so the greatest cost if an individual diet is commissioned – but they are usually readily obtainable from modest priced foods except when seasonable factors increase the cost of fresh foods. A garden or allotment helps keep costs low.

Recipes for a low budget

Soya beans are probably one of the cheapest sources of protein. The fastest and most economical way to cook them is in a pressure cooker. Unsoaked soya beans take about 45 minutes to 1 hour at 15lb pressure, but if you boil them on top of the stove, it takes 7–9 hours before they become soft. If you find eating soya beans gives you problems with wind, soak them overnight, then rinse well before cooking; in this case they will take 30–40 minutes to pressure cook. If you decide to soak them overnight, make sure to soak them in the refrigerator so they will not start to ferment and skim off the loose skins before cooking.

The basic method for cooking soya beans is:

400g (14oz) dried beans to 1.5 litres (2½pt) of water, with a tablespoon of oil or margarine and one teaspoon of salt.

There are many excellent recipes for soya beans in *The Farm Vegetarian Cookbook* by Louise Hagler (The Book Publishing Company). Here is just one of them:

SOYA FRITTERS
Cook 400g (14oz) dried soya beans, drain and save the juice. Measure 3 cups cooked beans and mash. Combine with the mashed beans:
1½ cups soya bean juice
1 cup whole cooked soya beans
225g (8oz) flour

1½ tbsp baking powder
1 tbsp salt
1½ tsp garlic powder
2 medium onions, peeled and chopped

Makes 3–3½ dozen

The batter will be like a thick paste. Drop by spoonfuls into the hot oil. Deep fry, turn so fritters brown on both sides. If the batter does not hold shape, add more liquid and more flour to the mixture.

Serve hot with:

Yogurt sour cream
1 cup Quark
2 tbsp oil
4 tsp fresh lemon juice or vinegar
Sweetener to taste
¼ tsp salt

Place ingredients in a blender until smooth. Pour into a dish and chill.

SOYA BEAN CASSEROLE
1 slice of salt pork or 2/3 rashers of bacon cut into strips
1 green pepper, chopped
1 onion, chopped
1 clove of garlic, chopped
2 tbsp butter
2 tbsp wholemeal flour
300ml (½pt) milk
100g (4oz) cooked soya beans
Salt and pepper

Serves 4

Brown the pork or bacon gently in a frying pan. Add the vegetables and garlic and fry until soft but still firm. Then make a white sauce using the butter, flour and milk. Put the cooked soya beans in an oven-proof dish. Add the meat and vegetable mixture to the beans and pour over the white sauce. Season to taste, then bake in the oven at 350°F/180°C, gas mark 4 for one hour.

The cheapest sources of meat protein are ox liver, which has a strong flavour and is often tough, so is best used in casseroles or stews, and pigs' liver which is also better in casseroles, stewed or used in curries rather than fried or grilled. One of the very best sources of meat protein is heart, which most people think they dislike although they have never tried it. Why don't you give it a try and see how good it can be?

HEART CASSEROLE
1 ox heart, 1–1.5kg(2¼–3lb)
3 tbsp oil
2 onions, peeled and sliced
3 level tbsp wholemeal flour
300 (½pt) stock
Salt and pepper
225g (½lb) carrots, peeled and grated
½ small swede, peeled and grated
Tin of tomatoes

Serves 4

Cut the heart into 1cm (½in) slices, removing the tubes, and wash well. Fry the meat in the oil until lightly browned and then place in a casserole. Fry the onions and add to the casserole. Drain off some of the fat, then add the flour and return to the heat for 2 minutes. Slowly pour in the stock and bring to the boil. Simmer for 3 minutes and then strain over the meat in the casserole.

Cover and cook slowly in the oven at 300°F/150°C, gas mark 2 for about 4 hours, adding the carrots and swede after 2½–3 hours. Add the tin of tomatoes to the casserole about 15 minutes before the cooking time is completed.

Note: For those concerned about losing weight, this recipe can be adapted by leaving out the flour and oil and browning the slices of heart in a non-stick frying pan with just a dribble of oil. The whole casserole can then be thickened if necessary with oat bran at the end of the cooking time.

LIVER CASSEROLE
450g (1lb) ox liver, sliced
2 level tbsp wholemeal flour
100g (4oz) streaky bacon, rind removed

2 onions, peeled and sliced
2 green peppers, seeds removed and thinly sliced
225g (8oz) tinned tomatoes
Salt and pepper

Serves 4

Coat each slice of liver with flour. Fry the bacon until crisp (in its own fat), drain, cut into small pieces and put to one side. Using about 3 tbsp of the bacon fat (keep the rest of the fat for later), fry the liver, a few slices at a time, until lightly browned on both sides. Remove the meat from the pan and put on one side.

Add 2 tbsp of the reserved bacon fat to the pan and lightly brown the onions and peppers. Drain the juice from the tin of tomatoes and add to the pan. Season to taste.

Place the liver on top of the vegetables, cover and cook for about 25 minutes until the liver is tender. Just before the end of the cooking time, add the tomatoes and heat through.

Serve sprinkled with small pieces of bacon.

LAMB AND BEAN HOTPOT
(This is a very quick recipe if cooked in a pressure cooker. If cooked in the oven, it will take about 2 hours.)

100g (4oz) haricot beans
4 pieces of scrag neck of lamb
2 tbsp vegetable oil
1 onion, peeled and sliced
Salt and pepper
Bouquet garni
150ml (¼pt) brown stock (made with a meat cube if necessary)
1 small tin red kidney beans

Serves 4

Pour boiling water over the haricot beans and leave them to soak for 1 hour. Trim the excess fat from the lamb. Brown the meat in hot oil (if you are using a non-stick pan, much less oil can be used). Drain off the excess fat. Drain the beans and put them in the pressure cooker together with the meat, sliced onion, seasoning and bouquet garni and the stock. Put on the lid and bring to High (15lb) pressure and cook for 20 minutes.

Reduce pressure in cold water. Stir in the tin of kidney beans and remove the bouquet garni.

This is excellent served with a green salad.

SPAGHETTI ALLA CARBONARA
225g (8oz) wholewheat spaghetti
2 rashers streaky bacon, chopped
1 small onion, peeled and chopped
Good pinch of oregano
Freshly ground black pepper
2 eggs, beaten
2 tbsp grated Parmesan cheese

Serves 4

Cook the spaghetti in plenty of boiling, salted water until just tender. While the pasta is cooking, fry the chopped bacon with the onion until the onion is translucent. Add the oregano and pepper. Drain the spaghetti, then add the bacon and onion mixture. Next stir in the eggs. Heat very gently until the eggs are just setting.

Serve immediately with plenty of Parmesan cheese sprinkled over the top.

WHOLE STUFFED CABBAGE
750g (1½lb) tin of tomatoes
Salt and pepper
150g (5oz) can of tomato paste
½ tsp Worcestershire sauce
Pinch of ground allspice
1 large cabbage
450g (1lb) minced beef
1 onion, peeled and chopped
1 clove of garlic, finely chopped (optional)
75g (3oz) cooked brown rice

Serves 6

Place the tomatoes and their liquid together with ½ level tsp salt, a little pepper, the tomato paste, Worcestershire sauce and allspice in a pan. Bring to the boil, stirring. Reduce heat, cover and simmer for about 20 minutes, stirring occasionally.

Remove the outer leaves from the cabbage. Cut out the stems of two large leaves and keep them on one side. Cut out the stem and centre of the cabbage, leaving approximately a 2.5cm (1in) thick shell. Discard the hard core and chop up the rest of the cabbage removed from the middle.

Place the beef, onion, garlic, pepper, 1 level tsp salt and 75g (3oz) of chopped cabbage into a large flame-proof casserole and cook for about 15 minutes. Add the cooked rice and 250ml (8fl oz) of the tomato sauce and stir to blend well. Remove from the heat.

Spoon the beef mixture into the cabbage shell and cover the top with the two large leaves put to one side earlier. With string, tie the cabbage so that the leaves are held in position. Pour ½ litre (1pt) water into the pan used for the beef mixture and stir well. Add the remaining chopped cabbage and tomato sauce and stir. Place the cabbage, stem downwards, in the sauce. Bring to the boil, then reduce the heat, cover and simmer for about 2 hours.

When ready, place the cabbage, stem down, in a heated dish, remove the string and spoon the tomato sauce over the top. Cut the cabbage into wedges and serve.

Here are some recipes for when you are entertaining and are short of cash.

Starters

LETTUCE SOUP
225g (8oz) lettuce leaves
1 small onion, peeled and chopped
25g (1 oz) butter
450ml (¾pt) chicken stock
Salt and pepper
300ml (½pt) skimmed milk
150g (5oz) carton natural yogurt (optional)
Ground nutmeg

Serves 6

Wash the lettuce leaves and put them in a pan of cold water. Bring to the boil, drain immediately and refresh the leaves under cold running water. Chop them. Cook the chopped onion in butter for 5 minutes until soft, then add the lettuce and stock and bring to the boil. Simmer gently for 10 minutes, then season with salt and pepper. Allow to cool, then sieve or blend the soup to a purée.

Add the milk and reheat gently. Stir in the yogurt if desired, pour into bowls and sprinkle each one with a little nutmeg.

CHOPPED LIVER
175g (6oz) chickens' livers
½ small onion, peeled and sliced
Salt and pepper
2 tbsp vegetable water or chicken stock

Serves 4

Place the liver in a small casserole and arrange the onion over the top. Sprinkle with seasonings and cover with vegetable water or stock. Cover and place in a baking tin filled with 2.5cm (1in) hot water. Bake in the oven 350°F/180°C, gas mark 4 for 45–50 minutes. Then mince the liver and onion and rub through a sieve or purée in a blender, adding all the cooking liquor.

Spoon into small pots and leave to cool. Serve with melba toast or slimline crispbread.

SMOKED MACKEREL PÂTÉ
225g (8oz) smoked mackerel, skinned and boned
100g (4oz) cottage cheese
¼ tsp cayenne pepper
1 tbsp natural yogurt
1 tbsp lemon juice
Black pepper

Serves 4

Combine all the ingredients together very thoroughly with a fork, or purée in a liquidiser. Serve with melba toast or slimline crispbread and a side salad.

Main courses

ROAST CHICKEN AND COTTAGE CHEESE
(*Taken from the St Ivel Cookbook*)
1½–2kg (4–4½lb) roasting chicken
225g (8oz) butter
1 small onion, finely chopped
225g (8oz) fresh spinach
3 heaped tbsp wholemeal breadcrumbs

Grated rind of ½ lemon
225g (8oz) cottage cheese with onion and chives
1 egg, beaten
Pinch of nutmeg
½ tsp salt
150ml (¼ pt) water

Serves 4–5

Remove the giblets from the chicken and keep on one side. Melt half the butter in a saucepan, add the onion and cook for 3 minutes slowly. Meanwhile, wash the spinach well, remove any coarse stalks and chop roughly. Add to the pan with the onion and cook both slowly for 10 minutes. Remove from heat and stir in the breadcrumbs, lemon rind, cottage cheese, egg and seasonings. Leave the mixture to cool, then use to stuff the centre cavity of the chicken. Spread the breast of the chicken with the remaining butter. Set it in a roasting tin and pour over the water. Place the giblets around the bird and cover loosely with foil. Cook for 50 minutes, then remove foil and baste chicken with the juices. Cook uncovered for a further 15–30 minutes, depending on size of bird. Discard the giblets and drain off the juices for serving separately. Season lightly.

STUFFED MACKEREL FILLETS
25g (1oz) butter
1 cooking apple, chopped
75g (3oz) celery, chopped
3 tbsp fine wholemeal breadcrumbs
½ tsp dried thyme
1 tbsp chopped parsley
Salt and pepper
1 tsp wine vinegar
2 large mackerel, filleted

Serves 2–4

Melt the butter and cook the apple and the celery until the apple is pulpy. Add the breadcrumbs, thyme, parsley and seasoning to taste, and mix well. Spread the stuffing on to the fish fillets, then place the fish in a lightly greased oven-proof dish. Cook uncovered at 350°F/180°C gas mark 4 for 25–30 minutes or until tender.

Serve immediately with a green vegetable or a salad.

LAMB WITH APRICOTS
½kg (1lb) breast of lamb, boned
½ small onion, chopped
450g (1lb) apricots canned in apple juice, chopped
Salt and pepper
Pinch ground cloves

Serves 2

Preheat the oven to 350°F/180°C, gas mark 4. Mix the chopped onion with the apricots and season with the salt and pepper. Spread the apricot mixture on the middle section of the lamb, roll up the meat and tie with string to secure. Sprinkle with salt and pepper and ground cloves. Wrap in foil and bake in the oven for about 1 hour.

POTATO AND YOGURT BAKE
¾kg (1½lb) potatoes, peeled and grated
Wine vinegar
300ml (½pt) natural yogurt
Pinch of grated nutmeg
1 small onion, peeled and grated
50g (2oz) Cheddar cheese, grated

Serves 4

Place the grated potato in a bowl of well-salted water, with a little wine vinegar. Squeeze the potato and mix with the yogurt, seasoning, nutmeg and onion. Place in a shallow oven-proof dish and sprinkle grated cheese over the top. Bake in a moderate oven for about 30 minutes.

Desserts

BAKED EGG CUSTARD
600ml (1pt) milk
3 eggs
Sweetener to taste
Ground nutmeg

Warm the milk in a saucepan, making sure not to let it boil. Whisk the eggs with the sweetener lightly in a basin and pour on the hot milk, stirring all the time. Put the mixture into a greased, oven-proof dish (or use individual dishes if you prefer) and sprinkle the top with nutmeg. Stand the dish in a shallow tin containing water and bake in the oven at 325°F/160°C gas mark 3 for about 45 minutes, or until set and firm to the touch.

FRUIT JELLY
4 tsp gelatine
3 tbsp hot water
Sweetener to taste
450ml (¾pt) orange juice, unsweetened
Fresh fruit of your choice, chopped

Dissolve the gelatine in the hot water with the sweetener, stirring until it is completely clear. Add the gelatine mixture to the juice and stir it in well. Chill to set. The fresh fruit should be added to the jelly as it is almost setting, so that the pieces stay dispersed. (Do not use raw pineapple or raw papaya – their enzymes will prevent the jelly from setting.)

APPLE AND MINT DREAM
4 medium-sized crisp eating apples, cored and chopped
6 sprigs of fresh mint
150g (5oz) natural low fat yogurt
2 egg whites

Blend the apples, mint leaves (save some for garnish) and half the yogurt in a blender until smooth. Mix in the remaining yogurt. Beat the egg whites until stiff and fold into apple mixture. Spoon into individual glasses, decorate with remaining mint leaves and chill.

ORANGE JELLY AND QUARK
1 pkt gelatine
450ml (¾pt) tinned orange juice
Low calorie Quark

Make up the gelatine with the tinned orange juice. When set, chop and mix with low calorie Quark and serve in individual dessert dishes.

6 'I've no time.'

Make time – that is our advice to anyone who appeals for help yet complains they have not got the time to follow the Eating Plan. If you have time to binge, then you have time to eat properly.

Compulsive eaters can find time to work, study for exams, look after their husbands and children and have hobbies and interests, yet many say they have not got time for the most important thing in their lives, getting their eating under control and being well again.

This is an extract from a letter sent to the Maisner Centre by an 18-year-old girl. It may seem surprising, but it is one of many similar cries for help we receive each week from 'busy' people.

> 'I am desperate for help. I feel suicidal and I am so scared that I will kill myself. My life is not worth living because of my eating. But at the moment I have not got the time to start the Eating Plan. Can you advise me what to do?'

You must change your priorities, then you will find time to get your eating under control. If you believe that life is not worth living unless your eating is controlled, then surely you can find time to do something about it. You will not live life to the full until you do.

An important part of the Maisner Method involves clients filling in daily food charts showing what they ate, where and when they ate and how they felt while eating. This provides vital clues to help us discover what may lie at the root of each individual client's problem. Yet so many complain: 'I do not have the time to fill in the charts.' If you have got time to eat, you have got time to fill in a chart, eat with one hand and write with the other.

There is no easy way out of the Food Trap, it takes effort – and it takes time. You have a choice between getting your eating under control or continuing to live in the trap, hating food and yourself. You also have the choice over how you spend your time. Think about the amount of time put into bingeing, from planning what to eat and buying it, eating it and resting afterwards. If you stopped wasting all that time you would be able to fill your life with so many interesting and exciting things. Don't be afraid of a future with time to spare, think of it as a challenge. There must be a hobby you have always yearned to take up; try anything, from horse riding to snooker, as long as it isn't connected with food.

Make time to sit down and compile a list of how much of the day you spend doing nothing constructive, such as watching television programmes you don't enjoy, that extra ten minutes in bed in the mornings when all you are doing is lying there thinking about getting up, or polishing all the furniture for the third time in one week. If you could cut back one thing on your list by ten minutes you could spend that extra time preparing some nourishing snacks to eat when you feel tempted to binge on chocolates and cakes. It only needs to be something simple, like mixing yogurt with fruit, or preparing a cheese dip and chopping up raw vegetables to go with it. That way you won't need to tell yourself during the day that you are eating a bar of chocolate because you did not have the time to get a protein snack. Be sure the nourishing snack is close at hand.

If you usually sit and watch television all evening, stop complaining that you never have any time. Switch the TV off, and ration yourself to watch only the programmes you really want to see. Try it for one evening and you will be surprised how much free time you find yourself with. As well as having time to prepare yourself a decent meal and get your snacks ready for the next day, you will find you have time to read a book, sort out your cupboards or write some letters.

Many compulsive eaters are insecure. They can never say 'no' to anyone and end up always busy doing things for others. These people want to please and believe that being at everyone else's beck and call is the only way to be liked. Instead, they usually end up being taken advantage of by others. If you are one of these people stop running around trying to please everyone else, you will find yourself a much nicer person as well as having more time to yourself. You will stop bottling up resentment and will no longer feel the need to give yourself those secret treats of cakes and sweets after feeling 'trodden' on by others. Please yourself; do only the favours that you truly do not mind doing because they will give you pleasure too.

Fiona always agreed to help out her workmates by doing extra overtime. She thought it made her popular and the money was welcome. But those extra hours made her tired and tense and she always binged when she got home. The extra money she earned was spent on food she binged and then vomited down the toilet. If all work and no play means your eating is out of control, weigh up the advantages. You may be earning an extra £10 a week, but it may cost you more than that in food, your health and happiness.

'I don't have time for breakfast.'

Then try getting up 10 minutes earlier. There is no excuse for skipping breakfast and just gulping down a cup of coffee before dashing off to work. It does not take any more time to eat a pot of cottage cheese, that is full of protein, than drink a cup of hot coffee. There are plenty of breakfast suggestions in Chapter Four.

'I don't have time at work for a mid-morning snack.'

If you have time to go to the toilet, then you have time to eat something. You are entitled to a break by law, so make sure you take it. Many people who use this excuse freely tell us that other people who work with them eat Danish pastries and doughnuts mid-morning. It may be easier for you to reach for a doughnut, but it takes as long to eat one as a protein snack, which will be far better for you. Plan your snack the night before or before you leave for work. You may find that your colleagues join you in a healthy break instead of eating their buns.

Two home-helps who work for the same local authority came to the Maisner Centre for help and both said they could not eat a mid-morning snack because of their jobs. Janette told us she did not have time for a snack because she was not allowed to eat on duty, but admitted she ate bars of chocolate in between visits instead. Louise said she could not keep to the Eating Plan because at every home she visited the old folk offered her a cup of tea and piece of cake or biscuit and she felt she could not refuse. Who was telling the truth? This example is one of hundreds we see at the centre of compulsive eaters deceiving themselves and others. We thought it was more likely that the women were offered a cup of tea and we told them to sit down with their host and instead of tea, eat your snack. No one would be offended; it is the company and the chat that the elderly people want anyway.

'I don't have time to cook a proper evening meal.'

Many women claim that they cannot face cooking when they get home from work; by the time they have done the housework, they are simply too tired to start work in the kitchen. Try finding time to do at least some of the chores in the morning before you leave for work. Save time by changing to a simpler hairstyle or make-up. Better still get up earlier. Get your family to help with the housework while you are preparing the meal, even if it is simple tasks like laying the table or hanging out the washing. If you have a choice between ironing your husband's shirts or preparing a nourishing meal, don't hesitate to cook that meal. Teach him to iron his own shirts or ask him to prepare the meal or hoover the hall while you do his ironing. Don't be a martyr to your family. They may protest at first, but if their help is going to help you get your eating under control, it is worth the battle.

Nourishing meals can be prepared in minutes following the Eating Plan. Keep the meals simple and cook something the whole family can eat. Don't waste time cooking something separately for yourself. You are not on a 'diet', you are sticking to a healthy eating pattern that your family can follow too and benefit from along with you.

Buy a slow cook-pot so that when you arrive home from work feeling too tired to cook, the meal is ready for you. This involves some foward planning and getting up 10 minutes earlier to prepare the meal and switch on the cooker. For busy people, pressure cookers and microwaves, which cut the time of cooking, are vital. You will feel more inclined to make the effort to cook if you know it will only take you minutes to sit down to a nourishing meal. Freezers are also time-savers. Keep a supply of vegetables and ready-cooked meals in the freezer for those occasions when you do not have the time to shop for fresh food.

Frozen vegetables are handy and there is nothing unhealthy about them. These days vegetables are packed and frozen within hours of being picked, unlike many goods at greengrocers which can be lying around for days. Unprocessed frozen foods are also fine, like chicken and fish.

Frozen shop-bought ready-made meals are expensive but keep a couple in the freezer for emergencies. Check the ingredients before buying; there is no need to get something that lists endless additives and sugar as there are many frozen products on the market which meet the requirements for healthy eating.

Keep a supply of foods that can be quickly and easily turned into a tasty and nourishing meal; for example, tins of tuna, pilchards and mackerel, which can be mixed with all sorts of ingredients, such as salads, baked potatoes and cottage cheese.

Here are some recipes that you might like to try. Each one offers a tasty, nourishing meal that all the family will enjoy but which won't take hours of hard work in the kitchen to prepare.

Recipes for quick, healthy meals

SPICY GRILLED CHICKEN
1 tbsp soya sauce
2 tbsp lemon juice
2 tsp mustard
1 clove garlic, crushed
2 small chicken breasts (approx. 100g (3½oz) each)

Serves 2

Mix the soya sauce, lemon juice, mustard and garlic to a paste and spread over the chicken breasts. Leave them in the refrigerator overnight to marinate. Preheat the grill to moderate and line the grill pan with foil and place the chicken on it. Then grill the chicken for about 8 minutes on each side or until the chicken is cooked.

Serve either hot or cold.

CHICKEN CASSEROLE
4 chicken joints
4 sticks of celery, chopped
2 onions, peeled and chopped
100g (4oz) button mushrooms
225g (8oz) carrots, sliced
1 glass of dry white wine (optional)
450ml (¾pt) chicken stock
50g (2oz) cottage cheese, sieved
Seasoning

Serves 4

Place the chicken joints, celery, onions, mushrooms, carrots and wine in a casserole dish. Mix a small amount of stock with the cottage cheese and then mix in the remaining stock. Add to the casserole with the seasoning. Cover and cook at 350°F/180°C, gas mark 4 for about 1¼–1½ hours.

LEMON BAKED FISH
750g (1½lb) plaice and haddock
15g (½oz) margarine, melted
1 tsp grated lemon rind
4 tsp lemon juice
Seasoning
¼ tsp dried basil

Serves 4

Put the fish in a shallow oven-proof dish. Combine the remaining ingredients and pour over the fish. Cook for about 25 minutes at 350°F/180°C, gas mark 4. Test the fish is cooked by using a fork to see if the flesh flakes easily.

These two recipes are taken from *The Sainsbury Book of Slimming* by Rhona Newman (Cathay Books). This is an excellent book crammed full of original and tasty recipes, nearly all of which are compatible to the Maisner Eating Plan. The two following ones require almost no preparation time at all.

MACKEREL WITH MUSTARD AND OATS
4 × 175g (6oz) mackerel fillets
2 tsp lemon juice
Salt and pepper
25g (1oz) porridge oats
2 tsp made mustard
Parsley sprigs
Lemon twists

Serves 4

Place the mackerel on a grill rack lined with foil. Sprinkle with lemon juice and salt and pepper to taste. Mix the oats and mustard together and spread lightly over the mackerel. Cook under a medium grill for 10–15 minutes.

Transfer to a hot serving dish and garnish with parsley and lemon twists.

HAM WITH PINEAPPLE AND YOGURT
4 × 75g (3oz) ham steaks
4 pineapple rings
150g (5oz) natural low fat yogurt
½ tsp made mustard
½ tsp yeast extract
Salt and pepper
2 tbsp chopped parsley
Parsley sprigs to garnish

Serves 4

Place the ham steaks in a shallow oven-proof dish and top each one with a pineapple ring. Mix together the yogurt, mustard, yeast extract and salt and pepper to taste. Stir in the chopped parsley and spoon over the ham and pineapple. Cook in a preheated moderate oven, 325°F/160°C, gas mark 3 for 20 minutes.

Garnish with parsley sprigs and serve with baked tomatoes if liked.

Fish can be very simply grilled or baked, and served with a lemon parsley sauce.

LEMON PARSLEY SAUCE
100g (3½oz) margarine
1 tsp grated lemon rind
3 tbsp lemon juice
1 tbsp chopped parsley

Combine all the ingredients in a saucepan until thoroughly heated, then pour over the fish – nothing could be simpler or tastier!

CHICKEN IN FOIL

(This is a good recipe as it leaves no washing up!)

225g (8oz) tomatoes, chopped
1 medium onion, peeled and chopped

1 small green pepper (optional), deseeded and diced
4 chicken joints
Salt and pepper
4 tbsp water or stock

Serves 4

Make four squares of foil, approximately 25 × 25cm (10 × 10in). Divide the vegetables equally into four and place on each of the pieces of foil. Place a chicken joint on top of the vegetables. Add a tablespoon of water to each parcel to keep the chicken moist, then fold over the foil so that it is firmly sealed. Bake in a moderate oven (350°F/180°C, gas mark 4) for about 35 minutes or until the chicken is cooked.

Serve with baked potatoes, which can be placed in the oven some 15–20 minutes before putting in the chicken.

CHICKEN YOGURT
4 chicken joints
50g (2oz) butter
2 onions, peeled and sliced
100g (4oz) bacon, diced
3 carrots, sliced
200ml (⅓pt) white wine or chicken stock
4 tomatoes, skinned and sliced
¼ tsp dried thyme
Salt and pepper
2 tbsp yogurt
Parsley

Serves 4

In a pressure cooker (with the lid off) sauté the chicken joints in the butter until browned on all sides. Remove and drain off the fat. Place the onions and bacon in the pressure cooker and gently fry until translucent. Then add the sliced carrots and place the chicken on top. Pour over the wine or stock and add the tomatoes. Season and sprinkle with thyme. Place the lid on the pressure cooker and bring to High (15lb) pressure and cook for 7 minutes. Reduce the pressure in cold water.

Place the chicken on a serving dish and pour over the cooking liquid. Top with the vegetables, then pour the yogurt over the chicken and sprinkle with parsley just before serving.

7 'I hate salads and vegetables.'

It is surprising how many compulsive eaters never eat fresh salads and vegetables. Instead, their mealtimes centre around refined food which has lost vital nutrients in processing. Fresh food is much healthier for you, as well as cheaper, than processed products, so make an effort to start eating salads and vegetables if you want to get your eating under control. Stop saying you 'hate' them, and you will.

Vegetables are useful sources of vitamins, minerals and fibre as well as containing small amounts of protein. The degree of nutrients they provide depends on their freshness and how they are cooked. Fresh vegetables are richer in nutrients than canned, yet frozen vegetables are sometimes more nourishing than fresh because they are picked and packed at their peak.

The most nutritious way to eat vegetables is raw. Salads are an excellent way of providing essential vitamins and minerals which are lost in cooking. Salads are useful to anyone with an eating problem because all those crunchy raw vegetables take a long time to eat, fill you up and contain roughage.

The best source of vitamins and minerals are found in dark green leafy vegetables, such as broccoli and spinach. Carrots, cauliflowers, green beans and potatoes are also useful sources. Vegetables also contain fibre and this is an highly effective way to avoid constipation – a common problem among compulsive eaters – rather than resorting to laxatives. Refined food does not make your body's digestive system work like fresh, natural food. Fibre is also a low-calorie way to fill you up.

'Salads are boring'

Compulsive eaters used to refined foods full of additives,

flavouring and sugar can find raw vegetables bland. It is a shock to their system to have to chew and munch their way through a plateful of crisp vegetables. But it is a matter of adjusting your taste-buds – and being adventurous. Salads do not have to mean limp lettuce, cucumber and tomatoes. And do not think of them as summer meals, basic salad ingredients are available all year round and add seasonal vegetables such as celery, leeks, beetroot, chicory, and red cabbage during the winter.

Use your imagination. You can add all sorts of things to a basic salad: mix in fruit and nuts and sprinkle beans, cheese or herbs and spices over the top. You don't have to use lettuce, but if you do, think of the different varieties – Cos, Webb's Wonder or Iceberg. Substitute cabbage for lettuce, try Dutch, savoy or red varieties, or experiment with Chinese leaves, spinach, watercress or beansprouts as your basic ingredient.

Forget traditional salads and make up interesting combinations of your own: cauliflower salad, tomato and avocado salad, green pepper and onion salad. There are no rules and regulations when it comes to making salads and the list of combinations is endless. Not all the ingredients need to be raw, cooked or marinated vegetables can make an exciting addition; try potatoes, courgettes, runner beans and broad beans.

Remember that salads are not necessarily 'slimming' if they are drowned in mayonnaise or rich dressings. Make your own which are just as tasty, lower in calories and free from chemical preservatives. If you are still doubtful about the taste of raw vegetables, make the dressing the central part of your salad and try something exotic and exciting: for example, orange dressing, by adding a freshly squeezed orange to French dressing; or experiment with herbs and spices, such as ginger or garlic.

'Vegetables all taste the same.'

That is not the fault of the vegetables, it is the way you prepare and cook them. Instead of boiling, experiment with steaming and stir-frying. Steaming prevents the nutrients from the vegetables being poured down the sink, which is what happens when you boil them in water. It is simply a method of cooking in or over steam from boiling water. Invest in a steamer or use a colander.

Stir-frying involves cooking finely chopped vegetables in an oiled pan over a high temperature. The idea is that the ingredients remain crisp and retain their texture, shape and flavour. It is a Chinese method of cooking, but there is no need to buy a traditional Chinese flat-bottomed wok; use a heavy-bottomed saucepan or casserole for the same effect. The key to successful stir-frying is to make sure that all the vegetables are sliced or chopped as finely as possible. Put those that take the longest to cook in the hot oil first, and then add the faster-cooking ones.

Start being creative and you will find endless ways to prepare vegetables. Don't think of simply dicing vegetables and plopping them in a pan of boiling water. Make a dish of vegetables more interesting by preparing them in different ways: chop them into full moons or ellipses, slice them diagonally into strips or cubes. Think, for example, of the variety of ways that a carrot can be chopped up, sliced into full moons, diced or cut into long thin strips.

Many vegetables can be cooked in more than one way, so why not start experimenting. For example, tomatoes can be grilled or fried, baked plain or stuffed, added to a casserole or eaten raw. For something simple, potatoes are so versatile: baked potatoes can be stuffed with all sorts of fillings: mushroom and cheese, sour cream and chives, bacon and yogurt to mention just a few. If you are feeling more adventurous, try combining vegetables with other ingredients: cooked celery with the juice and rind of oranges topped with chopped walnuts; Brussels sprouts with chestnuts; swedes cooked in rosemary and garlic. Make use of colourful vegetables to brighten a dish, like carrots, green, red and yellow peppers, red cabbage and sweetcorn. Use different vegetables for a combination of colours, flavours and textures, such as creamed swede with carrot, spinach and turnips, or peppers and onions.

Try seasoning vegetables with herbs and spices and experiment with combinations to make the simplest dish more interesting and appealing: add mint or parsley to peas; oregano, basil or onion to tomatoes; jazz up potatoes with paprika, onion or parsley; try a dash of vinegar or mint with greens; add nutmeg or lemon juice to green beans.

'I don't know what vegetables to buy.'

Don't go out to shop for vegetables with a set idea in mind, wait to see what is in season and looks the freshest. Stand in front of a greengrocer's stall and take a good look at the array of brightly coloured vegetables; there must be something that appeals to you. Don't be afraid to ask the greengrocer about varieties you do not know and how to cook them. Many greengrocers these days sell unusual and exotic varieties from overseas alongside carrots, potatoes and onions. Think beyond boiled cabbage and choose courgettes, aubergines, kohlrabi, okra or yams.

Buy only small amounts of vegetables at one time, so you are sure to eat them fresh. Leafy green vegetables lose many of their nutrients quickly – a few days storage reduces the vitamin C content of their leaves by up to 80 per cent. Always keep vegetables whole until you need them, don't wash, peel or slice them until then.

'But I don't know how to cook vegetables properly.'

Cook vegetables for as short a time as possible. Vegetables retain much more of their colour, flavour, nutritional value, shape and texture when they are steamed rather than boiled. More than 50 per cent of vitamin values in some vegetables and 77 per cent of mineral values are lost by excessive heating.

If you must boil vegetables, use the minimum amount of water and make sure it is boiling before you add the vegetables. Putting vegetables into cold water and bringing them to the boil harms the nutrients. Don't throw the water away after cooking, it contains valuable vitamins and minerals, so use it for stocks, sauces and soups.

Don't add salt when you cook vegetables. Many varieties contain a small amount of salt anyway and adding salt to the cooking causes a loss of nutrients. Spinach cooked in salted water loses nearly 50 per cent of its iron content compared to 19 per cent when cooked without salt. If necessary, add salt at the table.

Eat vegetables with their skins whenever possible, as much of the fibre and vitamins is found there.

There are so many varieties of vegetables and ways to cook

them that you must find something you like, if you try. After experimenting for a while, you will acquire a taste for vegetables, we guarantee it.

Tasty ways to cook vegetables

BAKED COURGETTES AND AUBERGINES

2 large aubergines
6–7 medium-sized courgettes
6–8 small onions, peeled
1 clove of garlic
Olive oil
Salt and pepper
Pinch of sweetener
3 tbsp sugar-free tomato paste
150ml (¼pt) stock
2 tbsp fresh wholemeal breadcrumbs
Olives to garnish (optional)

Serves 4–6

Slice the aubergines, sprinkle with salt and leave for half an hour and then rinse. Slice the courgettes and onions, and chop the garlic finely. Grease an oven-proof dish with oil, place a layer of aubergine in the bottom and sprinkle with salt and pepper. Cover with a layer of onions and garlic, and then a layer of courgettes. Carry on doing this until the dish is full. Mix together the tomato paste and the stock and pour over the vegetables. Sprinkle with the breadcrumbs and pour on 2 tbsp olive oil. Bake in the oven at 350°F/180°C, gas mark 4 for approximately 1 hour.

Decorate with a few olives on the top if desired, and serve hot or cold.

BRAISED CELERY

4 small heads of celery, trimmed and scrubbed
50g (2oz) butter
½ pint of stock made with a cube
Salt and pepper

Serves 4

Tie each head of celery with string so that it holds its shape. Fry gently in half the butter for about 5 minutes until golden brown. Place in an oven-proof dish, adding enough stock to cover half the celery, and add the remaining butter plus salt and pepper. Cover and cook for approximately 1–1½ hours in the oven at 350°F/180°C, gas mark 4. Remove the string and serve, pouring cooking liquid over as a sauce.

CHICKEN-FLAVOURED LEEKS
450g (1lb) leeks, washed and sliced
Chicken stock
White wine (optional) } to make up 300ml (½pt)

Serves 4

Just simmer the leeks gently for about 5 minutes, until still firm but tender, in either the chicken stock and wine for special occasions, or just in chicken stock on its own for every day.

HOT SLAW
1 white cabbage
2 eggs
4 tbsp water
2 tbsp lemon juice
Sweetener to taste
2 tsp dill seed (optional)
Seasoning
25g (1oz) butter

Serves 6–8

Shred the cabbage finely and cook in a little boiling, salted water. Beat the eggs in a saucepan, and then beat in the cold water, lemon juice, dill seed and seasoning. Warm slowly and stir in the butter in knobs. Stir until it begins to thicken, then remove quickly from the heat and pour over the drained cabbage. Serve immediately.

BROAD BEANS WITH ARTICHOKES
350g (12oz) frozen broad beans
200g (7oz) can of artichoke hearts
Juice of 1 lemon

1 tsp cornflour
Seasoning
1 tbsp chopped parsley
25g (1oz) butter

Serves 4

Simmer the beans for 5 minutes in boiling water. Drain and keep 150ml (¼pt) of the liquid. Drain the artichoke hearts and quarter them. Then beat the lemon juice with the cornflour, seasoning, parsley and butter into the liquid and heat in a saucepan until it thickens. Add the pieces of artichoke heart and the beans to the saucepan. Warm through and serve.

SPICED MARROW
1 onion, peeled and chopped
1 clove of garlic, peeled and chopped
1 tbsp vegetable oil
25g (1oz) butter
1 level tbsp paprika
1 level tbsp sugar-free tomato paste
Pinch of ground nutmeg
1 level tbsp wholemeal flour
Salt and pepper
150ml (¼pt) beef stock
4 large tomatoes, skinned and chopped
1 marrow, weighing about 1kg (2¼lb), peeled, seeded and cubed

Serves 4

Cook the onion and garlic in the oil and butter for about 5 minutes. Add the paprika, tomato paste, nutmeg and flour. Season to taste and cook for 1–2 minutes, stirring continuously. Pour in the stock and the tomatoes. Simmer for 15 minutes, then add the marrow pieces and cook for approximately 10-15 minutes or until tender.

GINGERED CARROTS

This is a recipe for carrots which makes them taste quite different.

450g (1lb) carrots, peeled and sliced

120ml (4fl oz) unsweetened orange juice
150ml (¼pt) chicken stock
1 tsp ground ginger
Salt and pepper
1 tbsp chopped parsley

Serves 4

Put the carrots in a saucepan with the orange juice and the stock. Add the ginger, salt and pepper and bring to boil. Reduce the heat, cover and simmer for 15 minutes. Drain off any excess liquid and serve sprinkled with chopped parsley.

Some fresh ideas for salads

TOMATO SALAD
Mix with sliced tomatoes a combination of any of the following:

Chunks of cucumber, parsley, onions, black olives, cubes of feta cheese, tuna fish or cooked green beans.

BROAD BEAN SALAD
Either serve broad beans raw if they are very young, or cook them very lightly first if they are slightly older. Combine them with a mixture of any of the following:

Sweetcorn kernels, haricot beans, kidney beans or peas.

PEPPER SALAD
Slice the pepper into rings or cut into strips, discarding the seeds in the middle. Serve the peppers either on their own with a dressing (some ideas for dressings are included at the end of this chapter) or add to a green salad. You can use red, green, or yellow peppers, and a combination of all three makes a particularly attractive salad.

RED CABBAGE SALAD
Finely shred and mix together equal quantities of red and white cabbage. Add either sliced apple or boiled chestnuts. You can also add grated carrots and/or onions.

WATERCRESS SALAD

An interesting and tasty salad is made if you mix together watercress – thoroughly washed – with orange slices and/or whole black olives. Serve with a dressing of your choice (see p.64).

ORIENTAL MUSHROOMS

Chinese cabbage leaves
225g (8oz) mushrooms, quartered or sliced
4 tsp sunflower oil
2 tsp lemon juice
2 tsp soya sauce
Pepper to taste

Chop the Chinese cabbage leaves and mix with the mushrooms. Make the dressing by combining the sunflower oil, lemon juice and soya sauce, then add pepper to taste. Toss the cabbage leaves well in the dressing.

ENDIVE SALAD

2 endives
Vinaigrette dressing (see p.64)
1 hard-boiled egg, finely chopped

Wash the endive leaves thoroughly in cold water and place in the refrigerator to chill. Before serving, toss the leaves in the dressing and sprinkle with the egg.

WINTER SALAD

2 eating apples, cored and chopped
4 stalks of celery, scrubbed and chopped
1 medium-sized cooked beetroot, peeled and diced
½ small onion, skinned and finely chopped
Salad cream
Chopped walnuts (optional)

Mix together the apples and the vegetables, and bind with salad cream. The chopped walnuts make a tasty extra if desired.

CARROT SALAD

3 large carrots, scrubbed
1 lettuce, washed

Vinaigrette dressing (see p.64)
Parsley, finely chopped

Grate the carrots and arrange on a bed of lettuce leaves. Add the dressing and sprinkle chopped parsley over the top.

MUSHROOM SALAD
100g (4oz) mushrooms
1 tbsp lemon juice
3 tbsp corn oil
1 tbsp chopped parsley
Ground black pepper

Wash the mushrooms gently without removing the skins. Discard the stalks, then slice them very thinly and place on a serving dish. Pour over the lemon juice and corn oil, sprinkle with the parsley, season with pepper, and leave for half an hour to marinate.

MARINATED ARTICHOKE HEARTS AND MUSHROOMS
400g (14oz) tinned artichoke hearts
350g (12oz) mushrooms
1 small green or red pepper

Dressing
2 level tsp salt
1 level tsp dry mustard
½ level tsp pepper
½ level tsp dried basil
1 small clove of garlic, crushed
Sweetener to taste
175ml (6fl oz) vegetable oil
120ml (4fl oz) lemon juice

Drain the artichoke hearts. Clean the mushrooms and slice them finely. Dice the green pepper, discarding the seeds. Make the dressing by mixing all the ingredients in a salad bowl until thoroughly blended. Then add the artichokes, mushrooms and pepper to the dressing and toss until the vegetables are well coated in the dressing. Cover the bowl and chill until required.

SPINACH, BACON AND YOGURT SALAD
225g (8oz) fresh spinach
50g (2oz) mushrooms
2 rashers of bacon
Pinch of mixed herbs
Yogurt dressing (see below)

Serves 4

Wash the spinach, being sure to drain it well, then tear into strips and place in a salad bowl. Clean and slice the mushrooms and add these to the spinach. Grill the bacon until crisp, then cut into small pieces. Mix the bacon and the herbs into the spinach and pour over the yogurt dressing. Toss well and serve.

Salad dressings

YOGURT DRESSING
225g (8oz) plain, low-fat yogurt
1 tbsp vinegar
2 tsp French mustard
½ tsp salt
Pinch of powdered sweetener
Pinch of cayenne pepper

Put the yogurt and the remaining ingredients into a jar, replace the lid, and shake vigorously until all the ingredients are well-blended.

BASIC VINAIGRETTE DRESSING
2 tbsp vinegar
Pinch of powdered sweetener
¼ tsp salt
Pinch of pepper
3 tbsp olive oil

Either place all the ingredients in a bowl and beat well until the oil and vinegar have blended, or put the ingredients in a jam jar, replace the lid and shake vigorously.

GARLIC VINAIGRETTE DRESSING
2 tbsp vinegar
Pinch of powdered sweetener
¼ tsp salt
Pinch of pepper
3 tbsp olive oil
1 clove garlic, crushed

Put all the ingredients into a bowl and beat well, or blend in an electric blender.

8 'I like cakes and puddings.'

Do you love sweet things more than you hate feeling fat and out of control around food? Remember that you always have a choice. If you want to lose weight and get your eating under control, then you must give up sugar, which does not mean to say you have to go without desserts and puddings.

Sugar is refined sucrose processed from the juice of sugar cane or beet. Despite medical warnings, we eat huge amounts, estimated at around a quarter of our daily intake of calories and in case of most compulsive eaters probably a great deal more. Many people are ignorant about which foods do contain sugar, including the obvious, cakes. Marion could not understand why she had an eating problem. She told us she did not eat flour, butter or sugar; in fact, she was not very interested in food at all. The only food she did enjoy eating a lot of, she said, was her mother's cakes (unfortunately I cannot supply you with the recipe!).

Mankind has always loved sweet tastes, but our primitive ancestors used honey and fruit to sweeten their food. Sugar cane is thought to have first been cultivated in the East from around 5,000 BC, and it was used for medicinal purposes and by the very rich as a sweetener. It was introduced into Europe around the twelfth century and although it was originally a luxury, it soon became available to all classes. In its present form, refined sugar has only been available for about 130 years, so in relation to our time on this planet, sugar is a new and unnatural substance and our bodies cannot cope with it, however much we might love the taste.

Refined sugar has been linked to many twentieth-century diseases, including heart attacks and diabetes, and blamed for hyperactivity and anti-social behaviour as well as tooth decay. Sugar can make you hungry as well as fat. The body only needs a small quantity of sugar and this it can get naturally from fruit, vegetables and milk. We do not need refined sugar.

'Chocolate gives me energy.'

Chocolate contains a large proportion of refined sugar, which does give you a lift, but don't be fooled, it is only temporary. A quick dose of refined sugar sends the blood sugar level soaring, that is when you may feel a surge of energy. However, the body compensates by rapidly releasing insulin forcing the blood sugar levels to drop. You shortly feel tired and hungry and can start to crave sweet things. It is a vicious circle.

The 1980s' trend for healthy living means that many people are becoming more conscious about what they eat, cutting down on too much salt and processed foods. But they appear to have a blind spot when it comes to sweets and chocolates. The excuse is that chocolate peps them up, just like the advertisements tell us. Our consumption of chocolate has grown by a fifth since 1981 and in 1984 we got through 448,000 tonnes, at a cost of £1.74 billion, far more than any other European country.

When people say they need sugar for energy it usually means they are addicted to the stuff. Children become hooked at an early age as their parents give them sweets for a treat or to comfort them when they are ill or hurt themselves. And people grow up equating sweetness with goodness and love, think of the terms 'sweet smell of success', 'honeybun', and 'sweet-heart'.

'Sugar is good for you.'

Refined sugar contains no nutritional value whatsoever. Also do not be fooled by sugar with fancy names; whether it is brown or white in colour, you can be sure that all the vitamins and nutrients will have been lost in the refining process and you will be left with nothing but a sweetener – and about 17 calories a teaspoon.

'I cannot give up sugar.'

It may seem impossible to resist your daily chocolate bar or cake, but your sugar addiction will gradually fade. Keep off sugar for as short a time as a week and you will notice the difference. You will begin to be aware of a greater variety of taste in your food because you are no longer smothering your taste-buds with sugar. Food which previously tasted sour, like some fruit, now tastes sweeter. And your eating pattern will improve as your blood sugar level stabilises.

Stop buying biscuits and sweets and you will stop being tempted to eat them. If you must have 'nibble' food around the house, keep a supply of fresh fruit and vegetables. Maureen told us that when she was bingeing an apple tasted sour, 'but when I got my eating under control I was amazed how sweet an apple actually is.'

Educate your sweet-tooth to enjoy natural sweets. Start eating fresh fruit for dessert and if you must buy tinned, look for brands using water and not syrup to can the fruit. Use sweet spices in your cooking, such as ginger, nutmeg and mace, to create sweet flavours without adding sugar.

However, even if you stop eating sweets you may be eating far more sugar than you realise, for it is hidden in many processed foods. Look in your kitchen cupboard and you will be surprised to find how many items contain sugar, from tinned meat to ketchup, from bread to toothpaste. That does not mean you must stop cleaning your teeth. Use your common sense to judge which foods to avoid and which contain such a small amount of sugar it would be more trouble than it's worth to ban it completely from your diet.

Some compulsive eaters become fanatical about sugar once they decide to give it up. From eating a daily dose of sugar in cakes and sweets, they will not touch any product containing sugar. Sallie refused to have a few drops of Worcestershire sauce in a glass of tomato juice because the sauce would contain a minute amount of sugar. Ellen scoffed at our suggestion that she use low-calorie dressings to liven up salads: 'They contain sugar, I could not possibly pour them over my food,' she said. Instead Ellen's obsession with her food and what to eat and what to avoid led her to bingeing on mounds of cakes, biscuits and bread. A bar of chocolate is made up of over half sugar plus 30 per cent fat, and should be avoided. But a low-calorie salad dressing that contains a little sugar but only totals 23 calories a tablespoon is acceptable. (The dressing also contains high-calorie oil, so the amount of sugar must be minuscule.) It is far better to eat a minute amount of sugar and learn to be relaxed about food, than continue to be obsessive about your eating and end up bingeing on cakes anyway.

Food packets may not list sugar in the ingredients or may even say 'sugar-free', but beware. The manufacturers may be disguising the fact that the food contains concentrated sugar, like dextrose or glucose. Steer clear of anything ending in 'ose', it is all sugar with a different name.

Watch-out for low-calorie packet puddings. These may only contain a few calories, but it is more than likely that most of these are from sugar and the packet contains few nutrients, yet bursts with chemical additives. The following ingredients were printed on one packet of low-calorie dessert: sugar, poly-dextrose, stabiliser E407, citric acid, modified starch, vegetable protein, flavour, sodium hexametaphosphate, colour E110, artificial sweetener (saccharin sodium). It doesn't sound too appealing, does it? Why not start making your own desserts? It can be fun, it does not take long and you can be sure they are chemical-free. Try making mousses and ice cream from gelatine and egg whites, or jelly from gelatine. They taste much nicer and are better for you and the family.

'I must bake for my family.'

Love is what your family needs, not buns. It is far better to be a happy mother and wife with no cakes for her children, than a misery with an eating problem who binges on the cakes she bakes, sometimes even before she has put them in the oven to cook. Try to work out what the real motive is behind your baking. Is it that deep down you know you will end up bingeing, but just cannot resist it? Don't torture yourself; stop baking immediately and don't put temptation in your way until your eating is under control. Be firm and don't let your husband bully you into continuing to bake for him. Take time to explain the effects of sugar and the effects that the cakes you bake have on your well-being. If he does persuade you to cook something sweet for him, use low-calorie artificial sweetener, which won't affect your blood sugar level if you succumb to temptation and tuck in too.

'I always bake for visitors.'

Start realising that nobody will take any notice whether you give them cakes or something else. If you once baked cakes for your friends or neighbours, try giving them a bunch of flowers instead, and when your mother-in-law visits give her a sugar-free dessert instead of a Victoria sponge.

'I have to keep sweets at home for the children.'

This is a feeble excuse for your own weakness. If the children are old enough to insist on sweets at home, tell them to buy their own with their pocket money – you can be sure they will eat them before they return home from the sweet shop. If the children are too young to have pocket money, you probably still have control over what they wear and what time they go to bed, so you should be able to stop them eating sweets too.

Daphne bought chocolate biscuits each day for her children's packed lunch at school, and always binged on the whole packet. We suggested that she leave the biscuits with a neighbour and her children could pick them up on the way to school. However it is far healthier to give your children fruit if they want something sweet, and it will be better for you too. Pat decided to start giving her children cheese and apples instead of sweets and biscuits. They enjoyed this new treat so much that it has changed their sweet-toothed habits and they now moan when they don't get their healthy snack.

'I have friends coming for tea and I must give them cake.'

Be adventurous and change the tradition of cakes for tea. Try cheese or avocado dips or a cheeseboard followed by fruit. Jane tried this experiment with her neighbours and to her amazement they liked it far more than cakes and sandwiches. Most women, whether or not they are compulsive eaters, are watching their weight and it will be a relief to see a plate of savoury munchies instead of sweet biscuits and cakes, which almost everyone finds hard to resist. Jane has successfully started a new custom in her street when it comes to entertaining.

'I have to eat my mother-in-law's cake.'

Face up to the fact that you have an eating problem, and you are using your mother-in-law's feelings to cover-up your own desire for wanting to eat that cake. If she knew that you would be so full of self-hate and guilt for eating it that you may throw it up in her loo, or take 50 laxatives when you get home or merely be in a filthy mood for the rest of the day, then she would surely want you to refuse to eat it. Explain to her that if she must give you something special when you visit, you would rather have a bunch of flowers, or perhaps a knitted sweater.

'I meet my friend for tea every day.'

Jill said: 'The temptation comes as soon as I walk in the tea shop and see someone else having a cream tea. I have to sit so I cannot see them or the cake display.' Stop torturing yourself. Meet in the park, an art gallery or at each others' homes rather than a café. If you must meet where food is served, choose somewhere which offers suitable food, so you will not feel guilty about eating. For example, a sandwich bar, where you can select a tuna sandwich on wholemeal bread, or a salad bar.

Sugar-free recipes for cakes and puddings

Compulsive eaters have a peculiar relationship with sugar; they desire it because of its taste, yet they hate the way it affects their health and happiness. While you are trying to give up sugar, experiment with artificial sweeteners that will not affect your blood sugar level. For example, try sweeteners with strawberries and yogurt, stewed rhubarb and ginger, home-made jellies and egg custards or a mug of hot all-milk de-caffeinated coffee. Remember that you are trying to lose your sweet-tooth permanently, so you do not face a constant struggle with temptation. But do use artificial sweeteners if you really feel that you want something sweet. You CAN live without sugar, you owe it to yourself to prove that you are sweet enough without it.

Many of your favourite recipes are adaptable to the Eating Plan: for example, one could make Summer Pudding, perhaps, by using wholemeal bread instead of white, and substituting sweetener for sugar.

LEMON MOUSSE
15g (½oz) powdered gelatine
5 tbsp hot water
4 eggs, separated
2 tbsp lemon juice
Grated rind of 1 lemon
Sweetener to taste

Serves 4

Dissolve the gelatine in the hot water. Beat the egg yolks lightly and add to the gelatine, together with the lemon juice. Stir in the grated rind and leave the mixture to cool. Whisk the egg whites until stiff and add the sugar substitute. Fold the egg whites into the lemon mixture and turn into a serving dish. Refrigerate until set. Decorate with lemon twists before serving.

Variation
Orange Mousse – use the juice and rind of an orange instead of a lemon.

STRAWBERRY DESSERT
2 tsp unflavoured gelatine
150ml (5fl oz) cold water
300ml (10fl oz) boiling water
275g (10oz) strawberries
Finely grated peel of ½ lemon
Juice of 1 lemon
50g (2oz) low fat dried milk powder
Artificial sweetener to equal 6 tsp sugar

Serves 2

Sprinkle the gelatine over the cold water and leave to soak for 1–2 minutes; then add the boiling water and stir until the gelatine has completely dissolved. Hull the strawberries, reserving 4 for decoration. Place the rest in a blender container, adding the rest of the ingredients, and purée until smooth. Pour equal amounts into dessert bowls, place in the refrigerator and leave until set. Halve the remaining strawberries and use to decorate the desserts just before serving.

PINEAPPLE VELVET

4 tsp gelatine
3 tbsp water
Sweetener to taste
300ml (10fl oz) orange juice, unsweetened
150ml (5fl oz) carton of double cream, lightly whipped
300g (11oz) can of crushed pineapple in natural juice
Toasted almonds, chopped

Serves 4

Make up the jelly using the first four ingredients. When it is on the point of setting, whisk until light and fluffy. Whip the cream lightly, then fold it into the jelly. Mix in the crushed pineapple and pour into individual dessert glasses to set. Decorate with the almonds before serving.

BAKED APPLE WITH RASPBERRIES

Next time you use the oven for roasting a joint or chicken, plan to try this super way of baking apples; serve them with natural unsweetened yogurt.

4 medium sized cooking apples
150ml (5fl oz) water
¼ level tsp ground cinnamon
Artificial sweetener to equal 4 tsp sugar
275g (10oz) raspberries

Serves 4

Stand the apples firmly on a chopping board, stalk-end downwards, and carefully core, removing the top two-thirds only. With a sharp knife, score the apple skin about a third of the way down from the top. Stand the apples in a shallow, oven-proof dish.

Put the water in a saucepan with the cinnamon and bring to the boil. Simmer for 1 minute, then remove the pan from the heat, add the sweetener and stir in the raspberries. Carefully spoon the raspberry mixture into the centre of the apples, pouring any excess over the top. Cover the dish with foil and bake in a moderate oven, 350°F/180°C, gas mark 4, for 45 minutes or until the apples are tender.

LEMON STRAWBERRY FLUFF
450ml (¾pt) water
Juice of 2 lemons
Grated rind of 1 lemon
3 tsp unflavoured gelatine
Artificial sweetener to equal 12 level tsp of sugar
Few drops of vanilla flavouring
25g (1oz) low fat dried milk powder
400g (15oz) strawberries, hulled

Serves 3

Place the water in a saucepan with the lemon juice and rind.
Bring to the boil then remove from the heat and leave to cool
slightly. Add the gelatine and stir until dissolved. Pour into a
bowl and leave until cold, then whisk in the artificial sweetener,
vanilla flavouring and dried milk. Chill until syrupy and
beginning to set, then whisk the mixture until thick and foamy.
Add the strawberries and stir gently. Pour into a serving dish or
a jelly mould rinsed in cold water. Leave to set.

RASPBERRY YOGURT FREEZE
225g (8oz) raspberries
2 tbsp water   ·
275g (10oz) carton of natural yogurt
5 sachets of artificial sweetener

Serves 4

Place the raspberries and the water in a saucepan, cover and
simmer gently until the fruit is soft and pulpy. Sieve the fruit
into a bowl and cool. Whisk the yogurt and sweetener into the
fruit purée and pour into a shallow container. Half freeze to a
mushy consistency, then turn the mixture into a bowl and whisk
until smooth. Return the mixture to the container and freeze
until firm. Transfer to the refrigerator about 1½ hours before
serving to make scooping easier.

COFFEE ALMOND ICE
4 tbsp + 1 tsp very strong decaffeinated black coffee
Sweetener to taste
2 tsp gelatine
Few drops of natural vanilla essence

2 drops of almond essence
300ml (½pt) low fat yogurt or a mixture of ⅔ yogurt, ⅓ quark
1 tbsp almond flakes

Serves 4

Turn the freezer to its coldest setting. Heat the coffee, dissolving the sweetener and the gelatine into it. Allow the mixture to cool, then add the vanilla and almond essences and whisk in the yogurt or yogurt and quark mixture, until smooth. Then stir in half of the almond flakes. Put the mixture into a container and freeze for about 3 hours. About 1 hour before serving, transfer the ice from the freezer to the refrigerator to soften. Then serve in scoops and decorate with the remaining almond flakes, lightly toasted if preferred.

RASPBERRY MOUSSE
225g (8oz) raspberries
15g (½oz) low-calorie spread
1 tsp lemon juice
15g (½oz) gelatine
1 tbsp of hot water (in a basin over boiling water)
150g (5oz) natural yogurt
1 egg white (size 3)
Raspberries to garnish

Serves 4

Cook the raspberries in the fat and lemon juice until a pulp is formed. Remove from the heat and sieve. Dissolve the gelatine in the hot water and stir this into the raspberry purée. Then stir in the yogurt. When the mixture is about to set, beat the egg white until stiff and fold into the raspberry mixture. Pour into a 600ml (1pt) mould and leave to set. Decorate with a few raspberries and serve.

HOT FRUIT SALAD
450ml (¾pt) water
3 cloves
3 cardamom pods, crushed
1 stick of cinnamon
Liquid sweetener

750g (1½lb) selection of fruit: apples, pears, plums, grapes,
   oranges
Juice of 1 lemon

Serves 4

Place the water and spices in a pan and bring to the boil. Cover,
remove from heat and allow to infuse for 15 minutes. Strain,
leave to cool and add the sweetener to taste. Peel and slice all
the fruit and add to the spiced syrup, together with the lemon
juice. Allow to infuse for a further 1–2 hours. Serve chilled.

SLIMMER'S SORBET
225g (8oz) soft, seasonal fruit
300ml (10fl oz) natural low fat yogurt
2 tbsp lemon juice
Liquid sweetener (optional)
4 tbsp water
15g (½oz) gelatine
2 egg whites

Serves 4

Keeping a few of the whole fruits for decoration, purée the
remaining fruit, either by pushing it through a sieve or in a
blender. In a bowl, mix together the fruit purée, yogurt and
lemon juice, adding the sweetener if necessary. Put the cold
water into a small bowl and sprinkle on the gelatine. Now stand
the bowl in a saucepan of water and heat gently until the
gelatine has completely dissolved. Now stir the gelatine into the
fruit mixture and leave to set. Beat the egg whites until stiff,
then fold them into the fruit mixture. Pour into a mould or
serving dish and freeze. Decorate with the reserved fruit before
serving.
Note Non-sweetened frozen fruit, such as blackberries or
strawberries, may be substituted if fresh fruits are not available.
Allow to thaw before using.

KIWI AND LEMON DESSERT
100g (4oz) Green Label Quark
½ lemon
1 egg white
2 kiwi fruit

Serves 2

Put the Quark in a bowl, grate in a little lemon rind and add the juice, mixing it together thoroughly. Whisk the egg white until really stiff and fold into the lemon Quark. Peel the kiwi fruit and cut off two slices. Chop the rest of the fruit and divide between two glass dishes. Spoon the lemon mixture over the top. Decorate with the slices of kiwi fruit and serve immediately.

FRUITY PEARS
2 sachets of artificial sweetener
1 tsp lemon juice
½ carton frozen concentrated orange juice, undiluted
2 large pears, peeled

Serves 2

Place all the sweetener, lemon juice and orange juice in a saucepan and bring gradually to the boil, stirring all the time. Add the pears and simmer for 15–20 minutes or until the pears are tender (you can add a little water if the sauce thickens up too much). Serve piping hot with natural yogurt or cream.

FRUIT CHEESE
225g (8oz) soft fruit (blackcurrants, raspberries or gooseberries are particularly suitable)
225g (8oz) curd cheese
3 eggs
3 heaped tbsp powdered milk dissolved in 300ml (½pt) water

Serves 6

Prepare the fruit, saving a few for decoration, then divide it equally between six individual oven-proof dessert dishes (adding artificial sweetener if necessary). Soften the cheese with a fork and beat in the eggs. Blend the milk into the cheese and divide between the dishes. Stand them in a roasting tin half-filled with water and bake in a moderate oven 350°F/180°C, gas mark 4, for 30–40 minutes until set.
   Chill before serving. Decorate with the whole fruit.

APRICOT CHEESE MOUSSE
220g (7¾oz) tin of apricots in natural juice

225g (8oz) curd cheese
Sweetener to taste
2 level tsp gelatine
2 tbsp water
2 egg whites

Serves 4

Using an electric blender or food processor, purée the apricots and juice together with the curd cheese and sweetener until smooth. Dissolve the gelatine in the water over a very low heat. Allow to cool, then stir quickly into the cheese mixture. Whisk the egg whites until stiff, and fold into the cheese mixture carefully. Spoon into four individual dishes and chill until set.

APPLE SNOW WITH HAZELNUTS
450g (1lb) cooking apples
1 clove
2 tbsp water
Sweetener to taste
1 level tsp grated lemon rind
Few drops liquid artificial sweetener (optional)
2 egg whites
15g (½oz) toasted hazelnuts

Serves 4

Peel and slice the apples, discarding the cores, and place in a saucepan with the clove and water. Cover the pan and cook over a low heat until the apple is soft and pulpy. Remove the clove and stir in the lemon rind. Taste and sweeten with a few drops of artificial sweetener if necessary. Leave to cool. Whisk the egg whites until stiff, then fold them into the apple purée and whisk again until fluffy.

Divide the apple mixture between four glasses, and decorate with roughly chopped hazelnuts. Serve within an hour.

ORANGE SORBET
1 fresh orange
175ml (6fl oz) natural unsweetened orange juice
225g (8oz) natural low fat yogurt
15g (½oz) powdered gelatine
4 tbsp water

2 egg whites
Sprigs of fresh mint (optional)

Serves 4

Grate the orange rind and add to the orange juice, then stir in the yogurt. Dissolve the gelatine in the water. Add the dissolved gelatine to the orange and yogurt mixture, stirring well. Leave the mixture until just beginning to thicken and set, then beat the egg whites until stiff and fold into the orange mixture. Pour the mixture into a suitable container and freeze. Peel the orange, remove the pith and cut into segments. Scoop or spoon the sorbet into tall glasses, with alternate layers of orange segments.
    Garnish with fresh mint.

LOW-CALORIE ICE CREAM
55g (2oz) dried milk powder
50ml (2fl oz) low-calorie fruit drink (of your own choice)
2 eggs
300ml (½pt) water
Artificial liquid sweetener
1 orange, divided into segments

Serves 2

Whisk the milk powder, fruit drink, eggs, water and liquid sweetener together until very frothy. Pour into ice-cube trays and put in the freezing section of the refrigerator until just beginning to set. Take out and put into a bowl and whisk. Freeze again until beginning to harden, then whisk once more. Add the orange segments and pour back into ice-cube trays. Freeze again before serving.

SPICED PEACHES
425g (15oz) tin of peach halves in natural juice
1 cinnamon stick
3 whole cloves

Serves 4

Place the peaches and their juice in a saucepan, together with the stick of cinnamon and the cloves. Bring to the boil and then reduce heat and simmer for about 10 minutes. Serve with cream or natural yogurt.

MOCHA MOUSSE
4 level tsp powdered gelatine
4 tbsp water
300ml (½pt) strong black decaffeinated coffee (cooled)
Liquid sweetener to taste
2 tbsp lemon juice
2 egg whites

Serves 4

Sprinkle the gelatine over the water in a small basin standing in a pan of hot water and stir gently until dissolved. Remove from heat and stir into the coffee with the sweetener and the lemon juice. Put in the refrigerator until it is just beginning to set and has the consistency of egg whites, then beat well until light and foamy. Whisk the egg whites until they are stiff and add to the coffee mixture. Continue beating until the mixture holds its shape. Pour into individual glass dishes and chill before serving.

When your eating is completely under control, perhaps you can start baking again, and here are a couple of recipes that won't affect your blood sugar level and have no sugar in them. Both these recipes have come from *The New Cookbook*, by Miriam Polunin (Macdonald & Co.). I have adapted the first recipe for coffee eclairs as Miriam Polunin has recommended the use of honey, which is unsuitable for compulsive eaters.

COFFEE ECLAIRS
75g (3oz) plain wholemeal flour
50g (2oz) butter
150ml (¼pt) water
2 standard eggs

Sieve the flour on to a plate. Heat the oven to 425°F/220°C, gas mark 7. In a medium-sized saucepan, bring the butter and the water to the boil. Remove from the heat immediately. Quickly tip all the flour into the pan. Beat well with a wooden spoon until the mixture forms a smooth ball that leaves the sides of the pan clean. Allow the mixture to cool slightly.

Grease a baking or an eclair tin. Beat the eggs together, add to the mixture in the pan, a little at a time, beating continuously to prevent any lumps. When all the egg has been added, the paste should look smooth and glossy.

Pipe out the mixture in 3–10cm (1½–4in) lengths, using a piping bag with a 1–1.5cm (½–¾in) nozzle. Bake for about 30 minutes. Remove the tin from the oven and slit eclairs along their sides to let the steam escape. Return to oven for 3 to 4 minutes. Place on a rack to cool.

Filling
Dissolve 1 tsp decaffeinated instant coffee in ½ tsp vanilla essence and a little yogurt and blend with 100g (4oz) low fat cheese. Add artificial sweetener to taste.

If you wish to have a creamier filling, mix 50g (2oz) whipped double cream with half of the above mixture.

SCONES
225g (8oz) plain wholemeal flour
Pinch of salt
4 tsp baking powder or ½ tsp bicarbonate of soda and 1 tsp cream of tartar
40g (1½oz) soft margarine or butter
Approx. 150ml (¼pt) skimmed milk

Heat the oven to its highest temperature. Sieve together the flour with the salt and baking powder (or bicarbonate of soda and cream of tartar). Retain any bran left in the sieve for rolling out the scones. Rub the fat into the dry ingredients.

Add most of the milk, until the consistency is very soft but not wet. Transfer the dough to a surface dusted with bran and pat or roll out until about 2cm (¾in) thick. Handle the dough as little and as quickly as possible.

Shape the dough with biscuit cutters or a knife, transfer the shapes to an ungreased baking sheet, brush them with milk and bake for about 10 minutes. The scones are done when, if you squeeze their sides, they feel dry and firm, not wet or mushy.

OAT COOKIES
50g (2oz) margarine or butter
2 tbsp Sweetex
1 egg, beaten
75g (3oz) wholemeal flour
1 tsp baking powder
75g (3oz) rolled oats
2 tsp almond essence
Milk to mix

Melt the butter or margarine and remove from heat, then stir in the sweetener and the beaten egg. Add to this mixture the wholemeal flour, baking powder, oats and almond essence. Mix to a soft dough, adding some milk if necessary. Roll the dough out thinly and cut into rounds. Grease a baking sheet and place the rounds on it and cook at 350°F/180°C, gas mark 4 for about 15–20 minutes. Remove and cool on a wire rack.

NUT CAKES

50g (2oz) margarine
2 tbsp Sweetex
1 egg, beaten
2 tbsp milk
175g (6oz) wholemeal flour
1 tsp baking powder
50g (2oz) chopped nuts
2 tsps almond essence

Melt the margarine. Remove from heat and stir in the artificial sweetener, beaten egg and milk. Then mix the flour and baking powder together and add to the other mixture. Add the nuts and the almond essence.

Roll out the dough thinly and cut into rounds. Grease a baking sheet and place the rounds on it and cook at 350°F/180°C, gas mark 4 for about 15–20 minutes. Remove and cool on a wire rack.

OAT BRAN MUFFINS

250g (9oz) rolled oats
4 tbsp Sweetex
1½ tbsp baking powder
350ml (12fl oz) skimmed milk
2 egg whites
2 tbsp vegetable oil

Grease a 12 capacity bun tin. Either liquidise or blend the oats to a coarse flour. Combine with the artificial sweetener and the baking powder, then add the milk, egg whites and oil. Beat lightly. Add the liquid to the dry ingredients and stir until blended. Pour into tin and bake for about 20–25 minutes, at 400°F/200°C, gas mark 6 until lightly browned.

9 'I'm always hungry.'

Are you hungry for food – or something else? There are two types of hunger, physical and psychological, and there are many people who do not know the difference.

People who are physically hungry may simply not be eating enough. They may leave too big a gap between meals or eat insufficient amounts of fibre, which provides bulk, especially if they eat 'slimming' sachet meals instead of complete meals of meat, poultry or fish with vegetables. Others may suffer from low blood sugar or be sensitive to 'trigger' foods which set off a binge.

Compulsive eaters find themselves on a downward spiral of feasting and fasting. They lose the ability to let their bodies tell them when and how much to eat, and they no longer have any idea of what is a 'normal' portion of food at mealtimes. They miss breakfast, skip lunch and avoid supper, nibbling on crispbreads, cottage cheese and apples in between. No wonder they feel hungry and find themselves bingeing on packets of biscuits, cakes and loaves of bread. But the next day they return to their semi-starvation diet, and before long their self-control snaps again and they binge once more.

Many compulsive eaters complain that the Eating Plan requires them to eat too much. This is because they have not been eating sufficient on their 'good' days, which is probably the cause of their eating disorder in the first place. The plan recommends you eat more than you probably would on a 'good' day, but it does mean you will be eating less than you would on a 'binge' day. It is far better to eat slightly more every day to avoid bingeing at other times.

The type of food some compulsive eaters choose to eat can leave them feeling hungry. Clare's constant moan was 'I am always hungry.' Her daily diet was mainly sugary carbohydrates and refined food, such as breakfast cereals, biscuits and processed ready-cooked packet meals.

Sugary food lowers your blood sugar, making you feel hungry again shortly after eating. Refined foods, like white rice and white bread, do not make your body's digestive system work because all the fibre has been removed in the refining process.

We showed Clare how to cure her hunger pangs by cutting out sugary food to stabilise her blood sugar, and by eating sufficient low-calorie protein and plenty of vegetables and salad to fill her up and make her remain satisfied longer. We recommended that, in between meals, she reached for a piece of low fat cheese or fruit instead of biscuits. The Eating Plan specifies that you must eat three meals plus three snacks a day, which should be enough to ensure that you do not end up feeling hungry at the end of the day.

When Clare started to follow the plan, she complained of being hungry. This was because she was making the wrong food choices. Clare wanted to lose weight but she chose high-calorie food and because she ate too many calories at one meal she cut back on the rest of the days eating and found herself feeling hungry. For example, she chose to eat cream cheese at 125 calories an ounce compared to 27 calories for cottage cheese. Because the Eating Plan allows cream and butter she was tucking into these too. If you have a weight problem, you might as well face up to the fact that you are never going to be able to eat lashings of cream and butter if you want to be slim. You should give up eating them now to avoid a constant struggle.

'I cannot stop eating.'

Certain foods make many compulsive eaters crave for more food. Even after a three-course meal they complain of still being hungry, and obviously this is not true hunger. The feeling can be caused by eating a trigger food, which is a form of sensitivity. Many compulsive eaters find that if they eat a trigger food they cannot stop eating. Yet because these foods can be everyday items, people don't associate them with their eating disorder. The most common triggers are sugar, bread, muesli, dried fruit and, surprisingly, apples. Alcohol can also act as a trigger. Try to remember what you were eating before your last binge.

Eating too much can also make some compulsive eaters crave for more. If they eat a big meal, containing a substantial amount of carbohydrates, it can result in an excessive insulin response causing the blood sugar to plummet and creating a feeling of hunger, before they have even left the dinner table.

'I have to eat stodge to feel full up.'

You do not need to eat 'fattening' food, such as pork pies and suet puddings, to make you feel satisfied. You can easily feel comfortably full on low-calorie food that will not make you fat or affect your blood sugar. If you are following the Eating Plan correctly, you should not reach a stage during the day when you feel excessively hungry.

'I do not know when to stop eating.'

Remember it takes 20 minutes for your stomach to tell your brain that you have had sufficient, so try eating slowly. You can pack in an awful lot of food in the first few minutes of a meal, and once you have over-eaten the system seems to break down and the 'stop switch' appears to break down as well.

'I am always thinking about food.'

An experiment carried out in an American prison among men who had no eating or weight problem, showed that when their daily ration of food was cut down to 1,500 calories per day, not only did they think only of food, but they even stopped thinking about sex! This shows that if you are hungry you are always going to think about food, and thinking about food makes you hungry. That may sound like stating the obvious, but to people on a weight-loss diet food becomes an obsession. One of the main causes of compulsive eating is strict diets, which we do not recommend. You become obsessive about what you must eat each meal, weighing it and measuring it. Sticking to a rigid diet is not a normal way of eating. Everybody feels different degrees of hunger on different days; some days you may feel like eating more than others, and there is no simple explanation for this. But many people believe that if they are on a diet they should feel hungry all the time. They think they must suffer to slim so deprive themselves to the point where their will-power snaps and they binge. Follow the Eating Plan and you will become more relaxed about food and when and how much to eat. You should find a lot more interesting things to think about than food.

On the days when you do feel more hungry than others, simply eat another small protein snack taken with something bulky to fill you up. This will stabilise your blood sugar level and will take away your hunger at least for the next few hours. If you are suffering from 'mouth' hunger and feel the need to be chewing on something then eat sticks of carrots or celery.

The Eating Plan eliminates real physical hunger if it is followed correctly. You will be eating little and often and if you eat the right foods, and eat slowly, you will never be over-hungry.

The next step is to recognise why you may still want to constantly eat. It is harder to help those who are psychologically hungry. They are more likely to be hungry for love, affection, friendship or may be craving mental stimulation. Food appears to be more easily obtainable than love to compulsive eaters. A baby's first pleasure is eating and as we grow we still equate food with childhood and those feelings of comfort and security. Sweets and cakes were 'treats' for being good or to make us feel better when we were ill or hurt ourselves.

Many people in the caring professions, such as nurses and social workers, suffer from compulsive eating. Compulsive eaters tend to be caring, sensitive people who don't get back what they give to others and feel empty inside. They turn to food to 'fill themselves up' or in other words to nurture themselves.

Elaine, a nurse, came to the Maisner Centre to watch a special video tape designed to help clients to relax. She lay on a reclining chair and as I wrapped a blanket gently around her, she burst into tears saying that no one had done anything nice like that to her before. She was used to caring for others and was desperate for someone to show her some tenderness and consideration.

A woman rang a radio station phone-in programme on eating problems and said that chocolates were her only pleasure in life and she didn't see why she should be deprived of them. This woman was deprived of fulfilment and love, but she had substituted the pleasurable things in life in her mind for something she could easily obtain – chocolates.

Jane's eating had always been perfectly normal until her

husband began to refuse to make love to her. So she sat up all night eating cakes. Jane wanted love not food, but food became a substitute for affection.

Compulsive eaters must discover whether their hunger is physical or psychological. For those who are physically hungry, their eating is on the right road to being under control as soon as they begin to follow the Eating Plan correctly. Other compulsive eaters need to solve their lack of love and loneliness before their eating disorder can be controlled. Try to keep occupied and stimulated; take up a new hobby or join a club to make new friends and learn something new and you will stop thinking about food all the time.

Table 9.1 Clare – original diet low bulk

		Oz	Grams	Cals	Protein grams
ON RISING	Orange juice	3½	100	40	0.8
BREAKFAST	Slice of toast, medium cut, white	1½	42	100	3.3
	Butter	⅓	10	74	0.1
	2 back rashers of bacon, grilled	1¾	50	202 .	12.6
MID-MORNING SNACK	Plain yogurt	5	150	90	9.0
LUNCH	Bread, 2 slices, medium cut, white	3	84	200	6.6
	Butter	⅔	20	148	0.2
	Cream cheese	2	56	249	1.8
MID-AFTERNOON SNACK	2 Ryvita	⅔	20	60	1.8
	Cottage cheese	2	56	54	7.7
SUPPER	Steak (raw weight)	6	170	335	32.0
	Tomato	1¾	50	7	0.2
EVENING SNACK	Cheddar cheese	2	56	230	14.7
	Small apple	3½	100	46	0.3
		34	964	1835	83.5

This diet is very concentrated in calories –
Low in fibre – low in total bulk.

Just over
2lb of food

Table 9.2 Clare – improved diet high bulk

		Oz	Grams	Cals	Protein grams
ON RISING	Orange (or ½ grapefruit) (Fibre lost if juice only used)	3½	100	35	0.8
BREAKFAST	½ carton yogurt, plain	2½	70	42	4.0
	Fruit salad, fresh, no sugar	3½	100	40	0.5
	Oat bran	¼	7	20	1.0
	Egg, boiled: size 1	2	56	100	8.3
MID-MORNING SNACK	Slice of lean only ham	1	28	47	8.3
	1 slice Ryvita	⅓	10	28	0.9
LUNCH	Roast chicken	3½	100	148	24.8
	Large mixed salad, e.g. lettuce	1¾	50	6	0.5
	tomato	3½	100	14	0.3
	cucumber	3½	100	10	0.6
	celery	3½	100	8	0.9
	pineapple	3½	100	46	0.5
	An orange	3½	100	35	0.8
MID-AFTERNOON SNACK	Other ½ carton of plain yogurt	2½	70	42	4.0
	Fruit salad as at breakfast	3½	100	40	0.5
SUPPER	Plaice baked or steamed	3½	100	93	18.9
	Carrot	5¼	150	35	1.0
	Cauliflower	5¼	150	19	2.9
	Baked potato in jacket	7	200	200	5.0
	Large Bramley apple, baked	7	200	74	0.6
EVENING SNACK	Chicken soup homemade* (¼ recipe)	10	280	51	6.2
		84	2271	1133	91.3

Contains 2½ times the bulk – yet with calories to spare and protein galore!

---

* *Chicken Soup – four portions recipe*

	Oz	Grams	Cals	Protein
Chicken, meat only	3½	100	121	20.5
Carrots	5¼	150	35	1.0
Cabbage	1¾	50	22	2.0
Onions	3½	100	23	0.9
Celery	1¾	50	4	0.5
Water or clear stock to make 2 pints total (40 fluid oz)	40	1134	205	24.9
Herbs, seasoning to taste				
Per 10fl oz portion			51	6.2

Filling Dishes

CREAMY CHEDDAR CHEESE SOUP

50g (2oz) margarine or butter
1 medium onion, skinned and chopped
50g (2oz) wholemeal flour
750ml (1¼pt) chicken stock
750ml (1¼pt) milk
450g (1lb) cheddar cheese, grated
½ level tsp salt
Freshly ground black pepper
2 slices wholemeal bread, toasted and cubed

Serves 4–6

Melt the fat in a large saucepan, add the onion and cook for 5 minutes, stirring all the time, until they are transparent. Stir in the flour and cook for a few minutes, then slowly add the chicken stock and stir until slightly thickened. Add the milk and bring to the boil, stirring all the time. Rub the mixture through a sieve, or purée a little at a time in a blender. When smooth, return to the saucepan and bring back to the boil. Reduce the heat and stir in the cheese and seasoning. Heat slowly until the cheese has melted.

Serve with cubes of toasted wholemeal bread.

SPLIT PEA SOUP

1 ham bone and meat scraps from bone
450g (1lb) dried split peas, soaked overnight
2 carrots, peeled and sliced thinly
1 medium onion, peeled and chopped
1.6 litres (2¾pt) water
6 whole allspice berries
12 black peppercorns
Bay leaf
Salt

Serves 4–6

Place the ham bone, peas and the soaking liquid, carrots, onion and the water in a pan and bring to the boil. Tie up the allspice, peppercorns and bay leaf in a piece of muslin and add to the pan. Turn down the heat, cover and simmer for approximately 1 hour. Remove the herbs and seasoning. Take out the bone and remove any meat. Return the meat to the pan and heat through before serving.

CURRIED BEEF IN PITTA BREAD
450g (1lb) lean minced beef
50g (2oz) onion, peeled and chopped
1 green eating apple, cored and chopped
1 level tsp salt
1 level tsp curry powder
3 pieces wholemeal pitta bread
250ml (8fl oz) natural yogurt

Serves 6

Fry the beef and onion together, stirring until the beef is browned and the onion is transparent. Spoon off any excess fat. Add the apple, salt and curry powder. Reduce the heat, cover the pan, and simmer for 5 minutes until the apple is tender. Halve the pitta bread to make two pockets, and fill with the beef mixture.

Serve with the yogurt as a dressing to be added to the pitta bread sandwiches and a large fresh salad.

CASSEROLES
These are very filling and when served with a large helping of vegetables and/or a salad, casseroles have unlimited possibilities. You can either pop them in the oven the day before and reheat the following day when they will have an improved flavour, or they can be cooked in a slow cook-pot when you go to work in the morning and they will be ready in the evening. It is quite a good idea to cook large amounts of casserole and divide them into small portions and freeze for use on your busier days.

DIPS WITH RAW VEGETABLES
As the vegetables used are raw, these dips take only a little time to prepare, but a long time to eat! Cut up celery, carrots, cucumber, peppers or anything that takes your fancy into sticks for 'spooning' out the dip. Try any of the following combinations to make tasty nourishing dips, either for snacks or main meals. (The amounts given are for single portions.)

100g (3½oz) Quark
Flesh of ½ an avocado
1 tsp lemon juice

150g (5oz) natural yogurt
75g (3oz) tinned tuna fish
Ground black pepper

100g (3½oz) cottage cheese
1 onion, peeled and finely chopped
25g (1oz) stilton

100g (3½oz) curd cheese
1 tbsp low-calorie seafood dressing
50g (2oz) shelled prawns

BAKED POTATOES WITH FILLINGS

A good stand-by for hungry people is baked potatoes. A large baked potato, with a suitable protein-based filling and served with a large salad, will fill even the hungriest of tummies. Stuffings can include cottage cheese, grated Cheddar cheese, sour cream, chopped ham, corn, kidney beans, haricot beans, tuna fish, chicken – the choice is endless. Any of the stuffings can be mixed together, or mixed with celery, parsley, herbs, etc.

CHILLED PEA SOUP

25g (1oz) low fat spread
1 medium onion, peeled and grated
6 large lettuce leaves, shredded
450g (1lb) fresh or frozen peas
2 tbsp mint, chopped
1 litre (1¾pt) chicken stock
1 tsp sugar
Salt and pepper
2 tbsp natural yogurt

Serves 4

In a large saucepan, melt the fat and add the onion, lettuce leaves, peas, and half the quantity of mint. Cover and cook for about 10 minutes. Add the stock, sugar and seasoning, then cover and simmer for about 40 minutes. Liquidise and pour into a bowl. Add the yogurt and chill.

Garnish with remaining mint just before serving.

CREAM OF MUSHROOM SOUP
600ml (1pt) water
2 chicken stock cubes
175g (6oz) mushrooms, finely chopped
50g (2oz) onion, peeled and diced
¼ tsp dill weed
50g (2oz) low fat dried milk made up with 250ml (8fl oz) water
1 tsp Worcestershire sauce
Salt and pepper to taste

Serves 4

Mix together the water, stock cubes, mushrooms, onion and dill in a saucepan and simmer for 10 minutes, then leave to cool slightly. Transfer the liquid to a blender and blend until smooth. Return to the saucepan and add the remaining ingredients. Heat through, but do not boil.

WINTER SOUP
4–5 tsps Bovril
600ml (1pt) water
1 onion, peeled and chopped
1 carrot
1 turnip
1 stalk celery
3 sprigs parsley, chopped
Pepper

Serves 4

Dissolve the Bovril in the water and place a 150ml (¼pt) of this in the blender, together with the onion. Blend for a few seconds. Peel and chop the remaining vegetables and gradually add to blender. Place the puréed vegetables, remaining stock, parsley and pepper into a saucepan and heat for about 15 minutes.

PEA SOUP WITH HERBS
1 onion
1 stalk celery
450g (1lb) frozen peas

1 chicken stock cube
1 level tbsp dried mixed herbs
1 level tbsp mint, chopped
1 litre (1¾pt) water
Pinch of sweetener
Salt and pepper
2 level tbsp skimmed milk powder
2 tbsp oatmeal

Serves 4

Chop the onion and place in a saucepan together with the peas,
stock cube, mixed herbs, mint, water and sweetener. Season
and bring to the boil, then cover and simmer for 25–30 minutes.
Place in a liquidiser or food processor. Return to the saucepan
and bring to the boil, stirring, and simmer for 1–2 minutes. Add
the oatmeal.

VEGETABLE CRUMBLE
225g (8oz) carrots, sliced
225g (8oz) cauliflower, chopped
1 onion, peeled and chopped
1 red or green pepper, diced
100g (4oz) celery, sliced
1 small tin of kidney beans
1 small tin of tomatoes and juice
1 tbsp soya sauce

Topping
100g (3½oz) cooked brown rice
100g (3½oz) wholemeal breadcrumbs
100g (3½oz) grated Edam or Gouda cheese

Serves 4

Boil the carrots, cauliflower, onion, pepper and celery for about
10 minutes. Strain off the water, keeping 1 cup aside. Add the
kidney beans, tomatoes and juice to the cooked vegetables, then
stir in the soya sauce. Stir over a low heat until most of the liquid
has evaporated. Place in an oven-proof dish, then mix together
the rice, breadcrumbs and grated cheese, pile on top of the
vegetables and brown in the oven or under the grill.

MOROCCAN BEEF

2lb lean stewing beef – in about 1½" cubes
1 large onion – chopped
8 pear halves
1½ tsp grated fresh ginger
1 tsp salt
⅛ tsp turmeric
1 stick of cinnamon
freshly ground pepper
½ tsp butter
2 minced cloves of garlic
1½ tbsp lime or lemon juice
1 tbsp chopped fresh coriander (optional)
2 tbsp chopped pistachios or toasted almonds
lime or lemon wedges to garnish

Serves 8   Oven temperature 325°F/170°C, gas mark 3

Sauté the onion, salt, pepper, turmeric, ginger, cinnamon in the butter, in a heavy casserole dish, until glazed. Then add the beef and garlic and sauté for a further few minutes. Cover and bake in the oven for 1½ hours. Cut the pears into thirds and add these to the meat and bake for approximately 30 minutes longer or until tender. Add the lime or lemon juice to the pan and heat, scraping up the drippings. Decorate with chopped nuts and coriander and garnish with lime or lemon wedges.

PORK CASSEROLE

2lb pork (shoulder or loin cut into ½" slices)
¼ pint dry white wine
12 small white onions
1 tbsp wholemeal flour
pinch of dried oregano and rosemary
Salt and pepper
¼ pint condensed consommé
1 tbsp fresh chopped parsley

Serves 4   Oven temperature 300°F/150°C, gas mark 2

Trim the fat from the pork slices and melt in a heavy frying pan. (Clear any brown particles from the melted fat.) Brown the onions and pork in the melted fat and then put these into a medium size ovenproof casserole.

Leave only approximately 1 tbsp fat in the frying pan, stir in the wholemeal flour and cook this for a few minutes. Stir in the wine and soup slowly and simmer until the sauce is smooth and thick. Season to taste. Add the herbs and pour this sauce over the meat which is in the casserole. Cover tightly and bake for 2 hours.

PAPRIKA VEAL
2lb cubed pie veal
8oz wholemeal noodles
1½oz butter
2 large onions chopped
1 level tbsp wholemeal flour
1½ level tsp salt
1 level tbsp paprika
4 fl oz yogurt
Chopped parsley to garnish

Serves 6

In a large flameproof casserole melt the fat and brown the veal – a few pieces at a time – and remove them as they become brown. Lower the heat and add the paprika and onions and cook for about 10 minutes, stirring continuously, or until the onions are tender. Place the veal in the casserole and add 4 fl oz of water and bring this to the boil. Lower the heat and cover and then simmer for 1¼ hours until the meat is tender. Cook the noodles in boiling salted water for 8–10 minutes, just before the casserole has finished, make sure they are tender and then drain well, arrange on a heated serving dish and keep hot. With 3 tbsp of water blend in the flour and slowly stir this into the casserole. Cook, stirring until this is thickened and smooth. Stir in the yogurt and heat but do not allow this to boil. Spoon the veal over the noodles and garnish with parsley.

10 'I live alone.'

Single people at the Maisner Centre often tell us: 'I would find it easier to follow the Eating Plan if I had someone else to cook for.' While, at the same time, the flat-sharers and the married women say: 'If I lived alone, I would find it easier to follow the Plan, because I wouldn't have to think of the others.'

But remember, choosing to live alone or with others will not solve your eating problem. Whether you live in a bedsitter or a household full of people, it is still your choice what you eat.

Susan, a student, moved from a shared house to a single flat because she believed it would be easier to control her eating if she was alone. Instead, she has discovered she can cook anything and eat as much as she wants with no one watching. Her downfall is roast dinners; she buys a joint of beef, lamb or pork or a whole chicken and cooks plenty of vegetables, roast potatoes and gravy. There is enough food for six, but she eats the lot and then makes herself sick.

Jane persuaded her father to guarantee a bank loan so she could get a large mortgage for a three-bedroom house. She believed that living with lots of friends would mean that she would not have the opportunity to binge. Instead she secretly eats her flatmates' food. She feels guilty and depressed and, although she is yearning to live alone, she is tied to paying a heavy mortgage plus the cost of her binges.

I have lived alone and shared a home while I suffered from an eating disorder, and for me living alone was the easier way to control my eating. But many people would not agree, it is different for everyone.

If you have not chosen to live alone, do not see your predicament as a disaster, think of it as a challenge. You are lucky to have the choice to be alone or in company. There is no excuse for you to spend time alone if you do not want to; take up a hobby, join a club, go to evening classes, go swimming or to play badminton. Other ways to make friends fast are through voluntary groups or singles' clubs.

There are more opportunities to binge undisturbed if you live alone. And you have got more spare time to fill with eating, too, compared to women with a husband and children to look after. Instead of feeling sorry for yourself and consoling yourself with food, consider the advantages of only having you to think about. Stock up the larder with foods compatible with the Eating Plan; you have no family to use as an excuse to buy biscuits and cakes. You can eat your meals without any explanation about why you are missing out sugar or processed foods, and you can choose your eating times without having to think about others' wishes.

'I cannot be bothered to cook for myself.'

Many people become compulsive eaters because they live alone. Teenagers who leave home for the first time often know little about nutrition and eat badly – take-away meals, convenience foods and fry-ups make them over-weight. They try to slim and start on the spiral of feasting and fasting, struggling to keep to a diet of cottage cheese and black coffee while bingeing on biscuits and cakes when they are alone.

Cooking may appear a lot of fuss, bother and time if you are alone. But if you make an effort with other parts of your life, such as your appearance, job, relationships and housework, it is time you got your priorities right when it comes to food and eating. Follow recipes which are quick to prepare and serve and preferably can be cooked in one pan or under the grill, so there is not much washing-up. Invest in modern appliances to help you cook quicker meals, such as liquidisers and electric mixers. A microwave oven will enable you to sit down to a meal in a fraction of the time it takes to cook in an ordinary oven. You will feel more inclined to cook if you know it is going to take less time and it means you will be out of the kitchen faster and away from temptation. A slow cook-pot is ideal. It takes just minutes before you go to work to prepare a nourishing meal and it will be waiting, ready to eat at the end of the day. Make use of a freezer for single portions of suitable food, such as casseroles, fish dishes or mince, to eat when you have not spared the time to shop.

Find someone else who lives alone, a neighbour, friend or workmate, and cook for each other on alternate nights. You can still keep to the Eating Plan because it only cuts out unhealthy food, such as sugar and processed products.

'I am lonely.'

Loneliness is a major cause of single people becoming compulsive eaters. If your only company in the evening is the television and the fridge, it may be difficult to resist continually eating. So change your lifestyle. Make sure you keep occupied in the evenings, entertain friends, go to the cinema or join a club. There are no excuses for being alone as there are so many social activities to take part in, wherever you live. On the other hand, many compulsive eaters say they like to be alone because they do not want to be disturbed when they binge. They may be using their eating disorder to cover-up their loneliness. Make an effort to find new friends and you will discover that there are plenty more exciting things in life than food.

'I don't like eating alone.'

Make a special effort at mealtimes and set your standards high. Don't perch a tray on your lap; lay the table and invest in a pretty cloth and china to make it look attractive. It might be just you sitting there, but serve your meal properly and it will soon become a pleasing habit. Team up with someone else who lives alone and take turns cooking for each other.

'It's difficult shopping for one.'

Many foods are for sale in family-size portions, which causes problems for compulsive eaters who may be tempted to eat the whole lot in one go. Start asking the shopkeeper for just the amount you want, for example, 100g (4oz) of liver, half a cucumber, a quarter of cabbage or just a couple of tomatoes. Sometimes it may seem easier to buy a single portion of ready-cooked food – there are many low-calorie brands on the market, from chilli to fish. These are only acceptable in emergencies when you have not shopped for fresh food.

'I share a flat.'

Single people who share flats face special difficulties. It may be hard, but you must try to tell your flat-mate that you are a compulsive eater. Hopefully she will give you support and encouragement, and having someone to turn to when you feel low will help you to cope. Your friend may want to help in a positive way, in that case ask her not to leave sweets and cakes around the home. Tell her that out of sight means out of mind. If you eat your flat-mate's food when you are alone in the house, you will have to tell her sooner or later anyway. Think of the shame and embarrassment that will follow when you are faced with explaining where all her food has gone. Your flat-mate will see you as selfish, greedy and totally inconsiderate, especially if she has nothing left for supper. March yourself up to the bath, go out for a walk, go to the cinema or telephone a friend whenever you feel an urge to raid her food. Keep a stock of your favourite protein snacks in the fridge so you never need go hungry. It is going to be hard at times, especially when she offers you a cake or chocolate. Do not be tempted, remember that you have an eating disorder, she does not. Instead of going without and watching her every mouthful, have a piece of cheese or fruit. She will probably feel inclined to follow your healthy habit.

If you cannot cope with seeing your flat-mate tuck into those cakes and biscuits, consider sharing a flat with another compulsive eater until your eating is under control. Put an advert in the personal column of your local newspaper; we don't believe you will have any trouble finding someone.

Remember that there is no difference whether you are living alone or with other people. Compulsive eating will follow you wherever you are. At the end of the day you will always be living with yourself.

Table 10.1   Working girl's eating plan

ON RISING	Grapefruit juice
BREAKFAST	Smoked haddock and poached egg; Ryvita
SNACK	Celery dipped in fromage blanc
LUNCH	Ham and a green salad
SNACK	Glass of skimmed milk and a pear
SUPPER	Liver yogurt*, baked potato and spinach *or* Low-calorie frozen fish in parsley, baked potato and spinach Baked apple
SNACK	The rest of the haddock in cottage cheese

* See recipe on page 103.

Table 10.2   Vegetarian single girl's eating plan

ON RISING	Orange juice
BREAKFAST	Quick porridge oats (2 minutes to cook) made with skimmed milk or soya milk and with a few sesame seeds on top
SNACK	Hard-boiled egg and tomato
LUNCH	'Take away' jacket potato with cheese *or* Rice and kidney bean salad* 1 pear
SNACK	Curd cheese with ½ an apple, chopped
DINNER	2 tofu burgers^x Large mixed salad
SNACK	Sugar-free yogurt

* See recipe on page 106.
ˣ See recipe on page 115.

Cooking for one

If you live alone and are lucky enough to have a microwave, you have every opportunity of cooking fast, delicious meals. Apart from stuffed baked potatoes, you can easily heat the 'Cook-in-the-Bag' fish and meat dishes if you are in a hurry, or you can make your own tasty dishes.

SAUTÉED KIDNEYS
100g (3½oz) lambs' kidneys, skinned, cored and chopped
25g (1oz) low fat spread
1 onion, finely chopped

Melt the fat in a suitable dish with the microwave on HIGH for 30–45 seconds. Add the onion and cover and cook on HIGH for 45–60 seconds. Stir in the kidneys, cover and cook on HIGH for 4 minutes.

Serve on a bed of freshly cooked vegetables such as cabbage, carrots, cauliflower, etc.

FISH
Fish is wonderful in a microwave as it retains its moisture. You only have to put one portion of fish into a suitable bowl, sprinkle with fresh lemon juice and black pepper and cook for a few minutes on HIGH. Variations can be done with fresh tomato, tinned tomato, frozen or fresh vegetables, prawns, mushrooms, etc – in fact anything your imagination can come up with!

CHICKEN
Either ready-cooked or uncooked chicken can be cooked in exactly the same way. For example:

RAINBOW CHICKEN
1 ready-cooked chicken leg joint
½ packet stir-fry vegetables, frozen
Garlic (optional)
Salt and pepper

Place the vegetables into a suitable container and cook in the microwave on HIGH for a few minutes until they are just cooked, and then remove, and place the chicken on a plate and cook on MEDIUM for a few minutes until heated through. The vegetables will retain their heat if covered with cling film.

TENDALE AND PRAWN SPECIAL
50g (2oz) Tendale cheddar-like cheese
1 small onion
25g (1oz) mushrooms
2 level tsp cornflour

120ml (4fl oz) skimmed milk
75g (3oz) peeled prawns
Pinch ground nutmeg
Salt and pepper
15g (½oz) wholemeal breadcrumbs

Grate the cheese, chop the onion and slice the mushrooms. Blend the cornflour with a little skimmed milk. Heat the rest of the milk in a saucepan. Stir the blended cornflour into the hot milk. Add the onion, mushrooms, prawns, nutmeg and seasoning. Bring to boil and simmer for 4 minutes continually stirring. Remove from heat. Leave aside one level tablespoon of grated cheese and add the remainder to the sauce. Stir until the cheese melts. Pour the mixture into a small oven-proof dish. Mix together the breadcrumbs and the remaining tablespoonful of cheese and sprinkle on the top. Place under the grill and cook until golden brown.

CHICKEN LIVER PÂTÉ
100g (4oz) chicken livers
2 tbsp water
Pinch of mixed herbs
1 small onion, chopped
2 slices of wholemeal bread
50g (2oz) cucumber
1 tomato
1 stick of celery

Chop up the chicken livers and place them in a saucepan with the water, herbs and onion. Cover and simmer for 5 minutes. Remove from the heat and leave to cool. Drain off the liquid and mash the livers, adding some of the cooking liquid if necessary.

Serve with fresh toast and the cucumber, tomato and celery.

KIDNEY KEBABS
2 lambs' kidneys
2 tomatoes
½ green pepper
50g (2oz) mushrooms
Lemon juice
100g (4oz) cabbage, chopped
1 medium apple or pear

Core and quarter the kidneys. Cut the tomatoes into quarters and the pepper into squares. Thread the kidneys, tomato and pepper pieces and the whole mushrooms on to two skewers. Grill until cooked, brushing occasionally with the lemon juice.

Serve with boiled cabbage.

LIVER WITH MIXED VEGETABLES
120ml (4fl oz) tomato juice
1 chicken stock cube
225g (8oz) liver, sliced
50g (2oz) mushrooms, chopped
1 stalk celery, chopped
½ tsp mixed dried herbs
50g (2oz) peas
25g (1oz) onion, chopped
75g (3oz) carrots, chopped

Heat the tomato juice in a saucepan and crumble in the stock cube. Add the liver, mushrooms, celery and herbs, then cover and allow to simmer for 10 minutes, stirring occasionally. Cook the peas, onions and carrots separately. Place the liver on a bed of the cooked vegetables and pour over the juices.

TOMATO, ONION AND CELERY SOUP
2 tsp low fat spread
25g (1oz) onion, finely diced
75g (3oz) celery, finely diced
175ml (6fl oz) water
1 tbsp tomato purée
Pinch of mixed herbs (optional)
Salt and pepper

Heat the spread in a non-stick saucepan, add the onion and celery, and fry gently for 2–3 minutes. Add the water, tomato purée, mixed herbs, salt and pepper and bring to boil. Cover and simmer for about 20 minutes or until the vegetables are tender.

LIVER AND YOGURT
100g (4oz) lambs' liver, sliced finely
2 tbsp natural yogurt
15g (½oz) butter or margarine

Chopped parsley
Sliced mushrooms

Cook the liver for about 1 minute in the fat. Remove from the heat and drain. Cook the mushrooms in the remaining fat, add a little water if necessary. Return the liver to the pan and add yogurt and parsley. Do not boil. Serve with a green vegetable.

BUTTER BEAN AND TOMATO SOUP

1 onion
1 small tin of butter beans
120ml (4fl oz) water
225g (8oz) tinned tomatoes
½ chicken stock cube
Pinch dried tarragon and ½ a bay leaf
Pinch of sweetener
Dash of Worcestershire sauce

Chop the onion and place in a pan. Add the butter beans, water, tomatoes and stock cube, together with the herbs and other seasonings. Cover and cook gently for about 10 minutes. Remove the bay leaf, then purée the soup in a blender until smooth.

TUNA AND SPINACH PITTA BREAD

1 wholemeal pitta bread
1 small tin tuna fish
1 tbsp garlic mayonnaise
Salt and pepper
225g (8oz) cooked spinach

Slit the pitta bread to form a pocket. Drain the oil from the tuna fish, then mix the fish with the garlic mayonnaise. Season to taste. Mix in the cooked spinach and spoon into the centre of the pitta bread.

If you prefer the fish and spinach hot, either heat the mixture on a low heat for a few minutes, or place in a microwave on MEDIUM for 2–3 minutes.

SPANISH OMELETTE

2 eggs
½ tbsp oil

1 small onion, chopped
1 small potato, boiled and sliced
½ small green pepper, de-seeded and chopped
½ small red pepper, de-seeded and chopped
1 tomato, chopped
Salt and pepper

Beat the eggs and season with salt and pepper. Heat the oil in a
pan and fry the onion until just softened. Add the potato and
heat through, then add the peppers and the tomato and cook for
a few minutes. Pour the eggs into the hot mixture and cook very
gently until eggs are just setting, then place under a hot grill for
a few seconds. Serve immediately.

QUICK EGG SUPPER
1 egg
2 tbsp milk
50g (2oz) Cheddar cheese, grated
25g (1oz) cooked ham, chopped
Salt
¼ tsp chilli powder
½ tomato, sliced

Beat the egg and add the milk, cheese, ham and seasoning. Pour
into a greased shallow dish and place in the microwave on
MEDIUM for 4 minutes. Then remove and arrange the tomato
on the top and microwave for a further 1–2 minutes. Leave to
stand for 2–3 minutes. Serve hot with a fresh salad.
   If you do not have a microwave, this can be cooked just as
well in a small non-stick frying pan.

VEGETABLE PANCAKE
A mixture of any vegetable, but cauliflower and carrots are
particularly good. Put the chosen cooked vegetables into a
blender with 2 eggs and liquidise and then either put into a
microwave until cooked or make as an omelette.

VEGETABLE AND LOW FAT CHEDDAR SOUFFLÉ
50g (2oz) low fat Cheddar cheese
50g (2oz) carrots, cooked
50g (2oz) Brussels sprouts, cooked
1 tbsp skimmed milk

1 medium-sized egg
Pinch of mustard powder
Salt and pepper
Pre-heat the oven to 425°F/220°C, gas mark 7.

Grate the cheese. Put the carrots and the Brussels sprouts in a bowl with the milk and mash together. Separate the egg, then beat the yolk and add to the vegetable mixture. Stir in the cheese and add the seasonings. Whisk the egg white until stiff but not dry, and then fold gently into the vegetable mixture. Spoon the mixture into a greased, oven-proof dish and bake for 30 minutes. Serve immediately.

RICE AND KIDNEY BEAN SALAD
25g (1oz) brown rice
25g (1oz) peas, fresh or frozen
25g (1oz) sweetcorn, fresh or frozen
50g (2oz) pineapple, fresh or tinned in water
25g (1oz) tinned red kidney beans
Stuffed olives (sliced)
Vinaigrette dressing (see p.64)

Boil the rice in lightly salted water until cooked. Drain well. Cook the peas and the sweetcorn. Cut the pineapple into cubes. Drain the kidney beans and mix all the ingredients together in a bowl. Prepare the vinaigrette dressing, pour over the rice and beans and mix up well.

STRAWBERRY FOOL
100g (3½oz) strawberries, mashed
½ sachet sweetener
150ml (5fl oz) natural yogurt
1 egg

Mix the strawberries, yogurt and sweetener together. Separate the egg and whisk the egg white until stiff. Fold into the strawberry mixture and serve immediately.

COFFEE CHIFFON CUSTARD
1 tsp instant decaffeinated coffee
2 tsp skimmed milk powder
½ tsp gelatine

120ml (4fl oz) boiling water
½ egg yolk
1 egg white
Sweetener to taste

Dissolve the coffee powder, skimmed milk and gelatine in the boiling water. Beat in slowly half an egg yolk and pour the mixture into a basin. Place over a pan of hot water and stir until the mixture is fairly thick. Remove from the heat and add a little artificial sweetener to taste, then leave to cool. Whisk the egg white until stiff and fold into the coffee mixture just before it has set completely. Put in the refrigerator to set.

STRAWBERRY SOUFFLÉ OMELETTE
2 medium eggs
2 tsp artificial sweetener
Few drops vanilla essence
2 tsp water
½ tsp butter
50g (2oz) strawberries

Separate the eggs and whisk the yolks, sweetener and vanilla essence with the water. Then whisk the egg whites and fold them in carefully. Melt the butter in a small frying pan, then pour in the eggs and cook until turning brown and setting on the bottom. Place pan under a hot grill to cook the top. Remove from the heat. Place the strawberries in the middle, fold over the omelette and eat at once.

11 'I am a vegetarian.'

Surprisingly, about 50 per cent of the clients at the Maisner Centre are vegetarians. This astounds many people who believe that a diet free of animal products is a particularly healthy way of eating. Vegetarianism is healthy if it is practised properly, but it often does not suit compulsive eaters. Many people think that becoming a vegetarian means just cutting out meat and fish and eating vegetables; but take the case of Irene who said, 'I am a vegetarian but love bacon and sausages'! Many people become vegetarians for a variety of dubious reasons:

'I did it to cover up my cranky eating.'
'I am in love with my boyfriend and he is a vegetarian.'
'It means I can cook my own food at my parents' home and eat what I want.'
'It is the only aspect of my life that I have control over in my parents' home.'
'I wanted to be different.'

A lacto-vegetarian does not eat any products derived from the slaughter of animals, including by-products such as gelatine, aspic and lard. Vegans go one step further by not eating any products which involve the exploitation of animals, including dairy products and eggs as well as honey in some cases.

Vegans are the hardest group of people to help control an eating disorder, and lacto-vegetarians come a close second. Some became vegetarians to cover-up their eating problem; for others the problem began when they became vegetarians. In many cases, they simply fail to understand the basics of nutrition.

People who do not suffer from an eating problem eat a balanced diet of meat, fish, dairy products and vegetables. The majority of their vital protein intake comes from meat and fish. Many vegetarians do not understand the need to compensate for not eating meat and fish. If a plate of meat and vegetables is put in front of them, they will leave the meat, without realising that it is essential to eat other sources of protein, such as dairy products, eggs, cheese, nuts, soya and beans and pulses, to make up an adequate intake of protein.

Nuts, beans and pulses make up a substantial part of a vegan diet, but you need to eat three times as many portions of beans compared to fish to get the same amount of protein, and consequently double the amount of calories. For those who do not judge their daily protein intake, it is easy to slip below the amount of protein recommended in the Eating Plan.

Table 11.1 Vegan eating plan showing amount of calories necessary to make up protein needs

		Grams	Cals	Protein grams
ON RISING	Orange juice	100	35	0.8
BREAKFAST	Oatmeal	50	200	6.2
	Soya milk	200	102	7.2
	Chopped walnuts	50	262	5.3
MIDMORNING SNACK	Almonds	50	283	8.4
	Apple	100	46	0.3
LUNCH	Wholemeal bread	100	216	8.8
	Yeast extract	7	13	2.8
	Tomato/lettuce/cucumber/beetroot (25g/1oz of each)	112	23	1.0
MID-AFTERNOON SNACK	Peanuts	50	285	12.1
	1 orange	100	35	0.8
SUPPER	Jacket potato including skin	200	200	5.0
	Boiled sweetcorn	100	123	4.1
	Broccoli, boiled	100	18	3.1
	Carrots, boiled	100	19	0.6
MID-EVENING SNACK	Wholemeal bread	50	108	4.4
	Peanut butter	50	311	11.3
	TOTAL	1519	2279	82.2

Table 11.2 Diet for comparison with Vegan diet – similar
protein, but fewer calories

		Grams	Cals	Protein grams
ON RISING	½ grapefruit	100	22	0.6
BREAKFAST	1 egg (size 1), poached	56	100	8.3
	Mushrooms	100	13	1.8
MID-MORNING	Slice of roast beef	28	54	7.8
SNACK	Raw carrot, whole or cut into sticks	50	12	0.4
LUNCH	Tuna fish, canned in brine	100	120	6.4
	Low calorie coleslaw	50	27	1.0
	Lettuce	50	6	0.5
	Tomatoes	100	14	0.3
	Cucumber	50	5	0.3
MID-AFTERNOON	Codroe slice, canned	70	93	17.0
SNACK	Lettuce	28	3	0.3
	Celery stalks	100	8	0.9
SUPPER	Chicken, hot or cold, no skin, no fat	100	148	24.8
	Grated cabbage	100	20	1.7
	Grated carrot	50	12	0.4
	Green and red peppers	100	20	0.9
MID-EVENING	Half-fat Cheddar-type cheese	28	72	8.4
SNACK	(Tendale)			
	Apple	100	46	0.3
	TOTAL	1360	795	82.1

Note: This chart shows how few calories are actually needed to take in
sufficient protein. Obviously you will add more food in the form of extra
salads, vegetables and fruit. You can also include jacket potatoes,
crispbread and wholemeal bread if you can cope with them.

We are not recommending a high protein diet; small amounts
of chicken or fish along with vegetables and other protein foods
are all it takes to keep to the target figure. It is far better to eat
more protein than that suggested in the Eating Plan than too
little. An egg for breakfast every morning instead of the two a
week generally recommended will do you more good than
bingeing. Although a low protein diet may suit some people, it
does not suit compulsive eaters. If they do not eat enough
protein, they will not stop bingeing. I have never found an
exception to this rule since I opened the Maisner Centre.

It is vital that vegans plan what they are going to eat carefully as they do not get nourishment from the foods that others take for granted, such as fish, meat and dairy products. They must eat protein with every meal. Protein is found in high quantities in soya and in reasonably high quantities in beans, pulses and nuts and in lesser amounts in other foods, such as potatoes and wholemeal bread. There are many soya products on the market that can be adapted in all kinds of dishes, including beans, flour, milk and meat substitutes. Make plenty of salads with different combinations of fruits, vegetables and nuts. Prepare lots of soups of beans and soya and freeze or put them in the fridge to use for hot or cold snacks.

As many compulsive eaters who are vegetarians do not like cooking, or experimenting with new ingredients, there is not enough variety in their diets, and boredom is a common cause of bingeing. Vegetarian food can be exciting, exotic or simple, such as sweet and sour haricot hotpot, chestnut roast with sage sauce or leek and butter bean casserole, but instead many compulsive eaters prefer to sit down to a bowl of cabbage or peas or binge on bowls of muesli.

Many people, including compulsive eaters, become vegetarians because of the exploitation of animals in factory farming, yet continue to wear leather shoes, buy wool carpets and use make-up and other beauty products tested on animals. Others believe that vegetarianism is a healthier way of life, yet still smoke cigarettes, drink alcohol and binge on cream cakes. Working at the Maisner Centre it is not always easy to be sympathetic to people who lead this rather hypocritical lifestyle – and suffer from an eating problem.

Compulsive eaters can keep to a vegetarian diet successfully and not binge if they make the effort to eat enough protein. Problems start when they try to lose weight. To eat sufficient amounts of protein each day, their consumption of beans and nuts must be high, and therefore they are also consuming a high amount of calories, and so they cut down on their protein to avoid putting on weight.

Many compulsive eaters cannot physically tolerate being vegetarian. Their bodies react badly, they suffer from bloated stomachs and wind from eating beans, pulses and vegetables in large quantities. Steve is a strict vegan yet he lives in constant misery and discomfort because of what he eats: 'My stomach seems to be permanently bloated, it looks like fat but it is not. I am constantly embarrassed because I cannot stop passing wind; when it is really bad, I stay at home rather than go out and then I end up bingeing on biscuits and bread.'

The only answer for many compulsive eaters is to change their eating habits, at least temporarily, until their eating is under control. They must start eating chicken and fish, which are high in protein, if they want to get better. It may seem tough, but it can be done. A consultant at the Maisner Centre was a vegetarian for health reasons but she had to begin to eat chicken and fish before she got her eating under control:

'I had the choice of deciding whether it was healthier to eat fish or chicken or continue bingeing and vomiting every day. There did not seem any logic to being a vegetarian any more. You don't have to eat huge lumps of liver, just small amounts of chicken or fish are enough to supply the right amount of protein. It was so complicated before trying to eat enough protein each day, now it is so much easier.'

Sandra suffered from constant health problems when she became a vegetarian because all her friends were following the trend. Her periods stopped and she felt tired, lethargic and depressed. A series of tests at the hospital showed that not only was she anaemic but suffered from hypoglycaemia as well. She never ate anything before 2pm each day and then usually a bar of chocolate. Her mother brought her a weekly food parcel believing that she was not eating properly because she could not afford it. Sandra's fear of bingeing and getting fat meant she immediately threw away the whole box in a bin in the street near her home. Now she is finally starting to realise that her eating may be the root of her health problems. She has begun to eat fish.

'I used to think that a good day's eating was cups of coffee and diet coke, but then I binged on whole loaves of bread spread with tomato sauce. It is amazing how much better I feel since I began to eat fish. It will be a long time before I can face meat, but I know now that being a vegetarian just does not suit me. I have told some of my friends that I am eating fish. I thought they would be horrified but they have been really understanding. I suppose I was looking rather ill.'

Rachel is bringing up her young daughter as a vegetarian. Rachel is constantly on 'faddy' diets and her child will not eat vegetables or salads and instead sticks to a limited diet of baked beans, cheese and chips, but mainly biscuits, breakfast cereals, crisps and sweets. Rachel came to the Centre after a friend warned her that her daughter was likely to grow up with an eating problem. Rachel said:

'I don't seem to have time to cook a balanced meal each day. But my daughter is full of energy and does not seem to be suffering. She is just not interested in food. She hates the thought of eating dead animals.'

We explained that although children are robust, her daughter may well suffer when she is older. Her limited diet will bore her and she will turn to other foods to compensate, and these will probably be sweets and confectionery. Being fussy about food means you are not relaxed about what you are eating, and that can lead to bingeing too. Her diet of mainly 'junk' food may also affect her tolerance to sugar as she gets older. While she is young it is far better to invest the time and energy to help her enjoy wholesome, healthy food. We recommend that children should be allowed to make up their own minds about whether they will or will not eat meat and fish and the time for that decision is when they are older.

Many compulsive eaters admit that becoming vegetarian was a way of disguising their obsession with dieting. Veronica became a vegan when she started teaching yoga. She began to fast at least one day a week and her daily food intake was mainly raw vegetables. She said:

'I feel terribly guilty eating animal products. I won't eat dairy products and I cannot eat beans and pulses because they give me wind and make my stomach bloated. I always feel under the weather and I know I don't eat enough, but I am very calorie conscious and I feel guilty if I eat more. And yet I still find myself bingeing.'

Veronica's diet contained almost no protein, as the amount found in vegetables is low. A few pounds in weight must be worth the happiness and freedom from her obsession with food, not to mention a much flatter stomach!

'Meat makes me ill.'

Bingeing also makes you ill. If the thought of a butchers' or fishmongers' truly upsets you, try to find a friend or relative to shop for you instead. You can disguise chicken and fish in all sorts of dishes with your favourite vegetables, herbs and spices. Eating chicken or fish could make such a difference to your recovery that you should make the effort to eat it for a month to judge the effects. After that you will probably feel so much better that you will want to carry on eating it anyway.

'I cannot afford meat.'

Meat can be expensive, but so is the cost of being a compulsive eater. Tot up the cost of your binges on cakes, biscuits and sweets and consider the cost to your own well-being, health and happiness of your eating disorder. Chicken and plain fish, such as cod or plaice, are not expensive compared to a joint of beef or salmon steak. Small amounts of chicken or fish, added to other protein foods, are all you need for your recommended daily intake of protein.

'All my friends are vegetarians.'

That does not mean you have to be vegetarian too. If you honestly feel strongly about the slaughter of animals, then make the effort to eat a proper balanced vegetarian diet, and you will get your eating under control. If you are only a vegetarian because your friends are, then it is about time you put your needs first. A vegetarian diet suits some people, and not others. Your desire to get well again must overcome your fear of being different or upsetting your friends, before you can get your eating under control. If your friends truly care about you they will understand why you must start to eat chicken and fish. However much they love animals, surely to them your health is

more important. If they cannot see it that way, then they are not
much good as friends.

*'I only shop at health food stores so I must be eating the right
foods.'*

Just because 'health food' is printed on the packet, the food
inside is not necessarily healthy for a compulsive eater. These
shops are brimming with foods commonly responsible for
triggering binges, such as nuts, dried fruit, muesli and honey.
Vegetarians believe these products are healthy, but if they are
causing you to binge, then they are obviously not.

Vegetarian cooking

TOFU BURGERS

(Taken from *The New Cookbook* by Miriam Polunin)

350g (12oz) tofu (beancurd)
75g (3oz) rolled oats
1 large carrot, grated
1 onion, finely chopped
1 tsp fresh ginger root, grated finely
1 tsp dried mixed herbs, including basil or oregano
1½ tbsp soya sauce to taste
25g (1oz) wheat germ

Serves 4

Heat the oven to 375°F/190°C, gas mark 5. Making sure the tofu
is well drained (keep the liquid for stocks), mix all the
ingredients to a firm blend. Let the mixture stand for a few
minutes. Shape into 8 burgers, and dip each one in the wheat
germ. Bake on a greased tray for 15–20 minutes.

CHICK PEA WEDGES

(Taken from *The New Cookbook* by Miriam Polunin)

175g (6oz) chick peas
1 bay leaf

2 tsp oil
1 large onion, finely chopped
1 carrot, grated
1 stalk celery, finely sliced
1½ tsp curry powder
75g (3oz) wholemeal breadcrumbs
2 eggs
2 tsp mild wholegrain mustard
Juice of 1 small lemon or lime (preferably a mixture of the two)
½ tsp marjoram
½ tsp white pepper
Good pinch of sea salt

Serves 4

Wash the chick peas in a sieve under the tap, removing any little stones or sticks. Soak them overnight. Change the water and cover chick peas with fresh water. Add a bay leaf and boil for 10 minutes, then simmer for 1 to 1½ hours, until very tender, in a covered pan.

Heat the oil in a thick-based pan and soften the onion, carrot and celery, covered, for 10 minutes. Mix all the other ingredients in a bowl, with the onion mixture.

Drain the chick peas, reserving the liquid. Mash with a fork or potato masher until the mixture is fairly floury. Add to the other ingredients with just enough cooking liquid to make a moist, but not soggy, mixture.

Grease a thick-based, fairly small pan, about 20cm (8in) in diameter, and heat. Tip the mixture in and level it off with a spatula. Cook over a low-to-medium heat for a few minutes, then cut twice at right-angles to make 4 wedges. Use a slice to turn each wedge over, and cook for a few minutes on the other side.

Vegetarian dishes

ORANGE AND NUT RICE SALAD
225g (8oz) brown rice
600ml (1pt) water
Pinch of salt
50g (2oz) hazelnuts

8 radishes
50g (2oz) spring onions
2 oranges
8 eggs, hard boiled

Serves 4

Cook the brown rice in the salted water until soft – about 30–40 minutes. Chop the hazelnuts roughly and quarter the radishes. Clean the spring onions and slice up finely. Peel and de-pith the oranges, then slice and quarter them. Cut the hard-boiled eggs into wedges. Mix all the ingredients together in a large salad bowl. Serve with a dressing of your choice (see p.64)

COURGETTE AND EGG OMELETTE
75g (3oz) butter
225g (8oz) courgettes, sliced
100g (4oz) mushrooms, sliced
100g (4oz) soft cheese with herbs and garlic
2 tbsp milk
6 eggs
6 tsp cold water
Salt and pepper

Serves 4

Melt 25g (1oz) of the butter in a saucepan, then add the courgettes and cook over a gentle heat for about 5 minutes until softened. Then add the mushrooms and cook for a further 2 minutes. Place the cheese and milk in a saucepan and cook on a low heat, stirring continuously, to make a smooth sauce. Mix in the courgettes and mushrooms.

Beat the eggs with the water. Melt the remaining butter in a large frying pan and then pour in the egg mixture and cook it, tipping the pan from side to side to spread it around evenly. When the underside of the omelette is setting, add the courgette and cheese filling and cook for a further 2 minutes. Cut into four and serve straight from the pan.

VEGETABLES IN CHEESE SAUCE
450g (1lb) mixed vegetables
225g (8oz) Cheddar cheese, grated
4 tbsp milk

½ tsp salt
½ tsp pepper
1 tsp Worcestershire sauce
4 eggs, beaten

Serves 4

Boil the vegetables in a little salted water until tender. Place the cheese, milk and seasonings in a heat-resistant bowl and stand in a saucepan of hot water. Heat gently until the cheese has melted. Add the beaten eggs and stir until the sauce thickens.

Drain the vegetables and arrange them in a serving dish, then pour the sauce over and serve immediately.

VEGETABLE CURRY
225g (8oz) brown rice
600ml (1pt) water
Pinch of salt
450g (1lb) courgettes
2 medium-sized leeks
225g (8oz) carrots
1 cauliflower
600ml (1pt) vegetable stock
3 level tsp curry powder
4 level tsp tomato purée
450g (1lb) broad beans
1 green pepper, sliced
4 eggs, hard-boiled

Serves 4

Boil the rice in the salted water for 30–40 minutes or until the rice is soft and all the water has been absorbed. Wash and slice the courgettes, leeks and carrots. Divide the cauliflower into florets. Place the cauliflower, courgettes, leeks and carrots in a pan, together with the stock, curry powder and tomato purée. Cover, bring to the boil and simmer for 15–20 minutes. Then add the broad beans and green pepper, and simmer for a further 5 minutes or until the beans are tender.

Serve on a bed of the brown rice and garnish with wedges of hard-boiled egg.

STUFFED MARROW

25g (1oz) butter
4 onions, peeled and chopped
2 carrots, chopped finely
2 cloves of garlic
4oz cooked brown rice
100g (3½oz) grated Cheddar
225g (8oz) tin of tomatoes
Salt and pepper
40g (1½oz) wholemeal breadcrumbs
2 tsp chopped parsley
2 tsp sage
1 large marrow

Serves 4

Preheat the oven to 350°F/180°C, gas mark 4. Melt the butter in a frying pan and add the onions, carrots and garlic. Cook until the onions are translucent, then add the rice and cook gently for about 15 minutes, stirring frequently to stop the rice sticking. Then add the cheese and tomatoes and season to taste. Cook for a further 10 minutes. Mix in the breadcrumbs, parsley and sage and remove from the heat. Wipe the marrow, then cut lengthways and scrape out the seeds. Fill each half with the rice mixture, place in a baking dish and cover. Bake in the oven for 1–1½ hours.

12 'I'm going on holiday.'

Going on holiday does not mean you have to abandon the Eating Plan. In fact, it is an ideal time to stick to it. There can be no excuses for being bored, lonely or not having the time; instead you have all the time in the world to concentrate on yourself.

Use your holiday as a challenge to get your eating under control and not as an excuse for your failings. Most people, it seems, take it for granted that they will put on a few pounds in weight during their holiday as they indulge themselves with good food. Indulge yourself in other ways: buy yourself a new bottle of perfume to wear each day while you are away, take some new make-up colours and experiment, treat yourself to a manicure or pedicure. Concentrate on making yourself feel good; we all know that if you do eat a cream cake each day you will feel guilty and angry and will probably binge and ruin your holiday. Take your mind off food and set yourself a goal to achieve while you are away; it could be a tapestry or knitting pattern, a new book or something simple like collecting flowers to press or shells to make into trinket boxes when you return home.

The rule to remember when you are on the move is Plan Ahead.

The biggest problem you face when you are on holiday is knowing how you will be spending each day. You may find yourself on the beach, sightseeing or tackling a mountain top, so start the day the right way by having a substantial breakfast to stabilise your blood sugar level and give you the energy to see you through the day. In many other countries fish, ham, cheese and fruit are the traditional breakfast, an ideal one for compulsive eaters. Whatever you choose, make sure your first meal of the day contains plenty of protein.

There is no need to miss your daily snacks. Whether you are walking along a river bank, sunbathing on a beach, riding along in a coach, carry something that is easy to eat with your fingers; a packet of nuts, for example, or a wrapped portion of cheese, and you can get a glass of milk anywhere.

'I am travelling by air.'

Meals on aeroplanes are renowned for being tasteless, pre-packed and full of additives. A useful tip is to ring the airline at least 24 hours before your flight and ask for a diabetic meal. This will be compatible with the Eating Plan and much tastier than the meals served to other passengers, and there is no extra charge. Otherwise take your own food. Pack it in light-weight plastic containers so it does not take up too much room or weigh too much. Make sure you have enough food for all your snacks if you are going on a long flight. Flying can increase your thirst, so, instead of sweet drinks, ask for fresh orange juice or water.

'I am travelling by train.'

Railway stations and buffets serve just about the worst food available anywhere. There are no rules about not eating your own food on trains, so take a packed meal. Prepare food in easy-to-carry plastic containers for the whole family. It will un-doubtedly work out much cheaper than the cost of an unhealthy buffet meal. Pack sandwiches made from wholemeal bread for the children and your partner and take containers of the fillings for you, keep within the Eating Plan by choosing meat, poultry, cheese or eggs with a mixed salad, fruit and nuts. Instead of buying cans of sugar-loaded soft drinks, take bottled water or cartons of fresh fruit juice. Take fruit in place of chocolate bars in case you or the rest of the family feel peckish before the journey ends. Buffets do serve cheese on toast and many sell apples, which you could eat and still follow the Eating Plan, but you would be better off making the effort to take your own meal.

'I am travelling by sea.'

Most ferries serve suitable food for compulsive eaters, for example, salads and fish. There is also plenty of snack food, too:

cheese on crispbreads, plain yogurts, tuna sandwiches with wholemeal bread plus fruit. If you do not want to rely on the ferry, take your own food in plastic containers. It is perfectly acceptable to eat your own meal onboard, and it will probably work out much cheaper too.

'I am travelling by road.'

It has become a tradition when setting off on a long car journey to take a tin of sweets or barley sugar. This is because people mistakenly believe that sugar-filled sweets 'pep' you up. Sugar will give you an initial rush of energy, but this will rapidly diminish and you will be left feeling more tired and stressed than before you popped that sweet into your mouth. Instead, you should take some fruit, it won't take up much room and will be easy to eat. The energy fruit gives you will last much longer than sticky sweets, and it will leave a fresher taste in your mouth.

Most petrol stations these days sell packets of sweets alongside the fan belts and cans of oil. If you find it difficult to resist temptation, send someone else to pay for the petrol. If you are alone, try to fill up your car with plenty of petrol at one time so you don't need to keep stopping.

Remember that if you are keeping to the Eating Plan you are eating a healthy balanced diet and your blood sugar level should be stabilised, so there is no need to eat sweets or drink coffee to give you a pep-up.

Long journeys mean you will have to stop somewhere along the route for a meal. Don't be put off by the road-side café chains, many have moved with the times and serve food compatible with the Eating Plan alongside the chips and milkshakes. Travelling by coach you cannot be sure that the driver will stop at a suitable eating place; he may call in at a fish and chip shop or take-away hamburger. Do not rely on the driver, make sure you take plenty of food with you to eat on the journey, so you do not get hungry and tempted by unsuitable food.

Remember that if you do go without food for too long on a journey, it is more likely that you will binge when you arrive. If you find that your well-planned travel arrangements go haywire and you are left with no choice but a bacon butty at a railway buffet or a two-hour wait until you get home, be sensible. One of the Ten Commandments is that you must not be obsessive about food. It is better to eat that bacon sandwich than to binge on biscuits and cakes when you get home because you are so hungry.

'I am going camping.'

Plan ahead and prepare meals all the family can enjoy, including you. Take plastic containers of cold meat, tinned fish and plenty of salad ingredients, cheese and fruit. Do not pack food that is forbidden in the Eating Plan, like sweets, biscuits and cakes. If it is not in front of you, you cannot eat it. Food always tastes better outdoors and the fresh air will probably increase your appetite. Be prepared and fill yourself up with raw vegetables and fruit whenever you feel peckish.

'I am staying in a self-catering flat.'

Only buy food that is suitable for you. If there are no cakes or biscuits in the flat, you cannot be tempted to eat them. Stock up with plenty of food before you go, but make sure it is compatible with the Eating Plan. Go to the cash and carry and buy cartons of yogurt and tins of fish. Ensure that whenever you are hungry, the only food around is acceptable for you to eat.

'I am staying at a hotel.'

Book ahead and choose a hotel where you can check-up on the menu before you arrive. Hotel restaurants usually have something on the menu that is suitable for you, for example, grilled fish or salad. If all the dishes appear to be laden with cream, wine or pastry, ask for the main ingredient, the fish or the meat, to be served plain. Hotels are used to catering for customers with all sorts of diets, whether because of health or religion, and do not object to varying a dish. Remember that you are paying and the 'Customer is always right'.

If you are worried that once in the hotel dining room you will want to binge or that you will succumb to temptation and order the wrong food, eat something small but filling beforehand, such as cottage cheese or a low-calorie soup. Packet soups do not take up much room in your luggage and there are kettles to make drinks in most hotel bedrooms these days. These soups are not nutritious and they do contain a small amount of sugar, but it is better to drink them than binge on chocolate bars after your meal because you are still hungry.

With small hotels or boarding houses, check in advance what the menu is like. If it is mostly chips and suet puddings, ask the owner if she will prepare a separate meal for you. Tell her you are avoiding sugar and fried food for health reasons. It may be better to stick to bed and breakfast and go out for the rest of the day's meals to restaurants and café where you know you can get suitable food.

'I am travelling abroad.'

When you pack your suitcase you will not forget your toothbrush, so don't forget a tin opener, a knife, fork and a spoon too. This will ensure that you are well prepared to cope with your eating problem while you are away. Go to markets to buy fresh fruit, vegetables, ham, cheese and milk to eat in your hotel room for snacks in between hotel meals.

Remember, when you are on holiday, you should be having a happy, relaxed time. Everyone around you may be letting themselves go when it comes to eating and there is no reason why you should have to feel left out. The Eating Plan allows you to have strawberries with a dollop of cream, or avocado with giant prawns and other goodies. The trick is to find the happy balance between indulging yourself and depriving yourself. Prove to yourself that you can eat sensibly and still enjoy yourself.

When you get home you will more than likely feel marvellous, relaxed and full of beans. It could well be that the rest has done you the power of good. But think about whether it is because your diet changed for the better while you were away; perhaps you were not eating the food that normally triggers a binge, such as sugary cakes or muesli.

Holidays come round every year for most of us, you may want to avoid facing up to your eating problem this year, but what about next year? You will enjoy your holiday much more if you are in control of your eating.

Packed lunch and picnic ideas

When going on picnics you can take with you such things as poultry, cold cuts of meat, home-made burgers, tofu burgers, meat balls, and a variety of salads with the dressings packed separately, so that the salads will not go soggy before eating. You could also take, for example, either a meat loaf, such as Picnic Loaf, or if you are a vegetarian you could try a Nut and Rice Loaf.

Both these loaves can be wrapped in foil and frozen until ready for use, but will need to be thawed overnight in a fridge.

FRENCH-STYLE PICNIC LOAF
10 rashers streaky bacon, rind removed
750g (1½lb) minced beef
1 large onion, chopped finely
2 cloves of garlic, crushed (optional)
175g (6oz) fresh wholemeal breadcrumbs
1 tbsp parsley, chopped
6 small gherkins, chopped
1 tbsp French mustard
2 medium eggs, beaten
Salt and pepper to taste

Serves 8–10

Use the back of a knife to stretch the bacon rashers, doubling them in length if possible. Put two or three rashers on one side and use the rest of the bacon to line the base and sides of a 1.25 litre (2¼pt) capacity loaf tin. In a bowl mix together all the remaining ingredients thoroughly. Press this mixture into the tin and smooth over the surface. Cover the top of the loaf with the remaining bacon. Cover with foil and cook in the centre of a moderately hot oven for 1¼ hours on 400°F/200°C, gas mark 6.

Remove and cover with a new piece of foil and weigh down with a bag of sugar and leave until cold, then place in the fridge overnight. Turn out of tin and place in suitable container for travelling, or freeze for a future occasion.

NUT AND RICE LOAF
1½ tsp turmeric
225g (8oz) brown rice

600ml (1pt) water
Pinch of salt
50g (2oz) salted peanuts, chopped
1 red pepper, chopped
2 stalks of celery, chopped
1 large onion, chopped finely
2 cloves garlic, crushed (optional)
100g (4oz) mature Cheddar cheese, grated
1 tbsp Worcestershire sauce
2 tbsp tomato purée
2 tbsp horseradish sauce
2 medium eggs, beaten
Salt and pepper to taste
10 stuffed olives

Serves 8–10

Cook the rice in the salted water with the turmeric until the rice is soft and all the water has been absorbed. Line the base and sides of a 1.25 litre (2¼pt) capacity loaf tin with greased foil, leaving enough foil to stand about 2.5cm (1in) above the sides of the tin. Mix the cooked rice with all the remaining ingredients, except for the olives. Put two-thirds of the mixture into the tin, then press the olives lengthways into the mixture in two rows. Place the remaining rice mixture on the top, smooth over and cover surface with foil.

Cook in the oven at 350°F/180°C, gas mark 4 for 1¼ hours. Leave to cool, then place in the fridge overnight. Turn out of the tin and place in a suitable container for travelling or leave in the foil and freeze.

QUICK MEAT LOAF
This is a quick meat loaf which can be made in the microwave

25g (1oz) butter
1 large onion, diced finely
450g (1lb) minced meat
50g (2oz) fresh wholemeal breadcrumbs
1 tsp dried mixed herbs
225g (8oz) ready-made sausalata mix
1 clove of garlic, crushed (optional)
2 medium eggs, beaten lightly

50g (2oz) stuffed olives, chopped
Salt and pepper to taste

Serve 6–8

Place the butter and the onion in a large bowl, then cover for 5 minutes on HIGH. Stir in the meat, breadcrumbs, herbs, sausalata and garlic with a fork. Cover and cook for 5 minutes on HIGH. Stir in the eggs, olives, salt and pepper, then put the mixture in a greased 1.75 litre (3pt) soufflé dish. Cover and cook for 4 minutes on HIGH. Remove the cover and spread a piece of greaseproof paper over the top, then place a heavy object on the top to weigh it down. Leave the loaf to stand until cold.

Turn out and place in a suitable container for travelling, or freeze.

13 'Special occasions make it impossible.'

Compulsive eaters often say they cannot start the Eating Plan because Christmas is coming, or it's their wedding anniversary soon or their birthday next month. There are going to be events to celebrate every year. Start the plan today and you will discover you can easily follow it and still enjoy any kind of celebration, whether at home or out at a restaurant.

The plan allows a wide variety of food so there is no need to feel deprived or resentful that you are missing out. Be strong; do not eat what you should not, but don't be obsessive about your food, remember that you are celebrating, so relax and have a good time.

'I'm entertaining at home.'

You can make interesting, easy, luxurious or cheap meals to suit any occasion following the Eating Plan. Remember that the majority of women are watching their weight, so, like you, they don't want to sit down to meals laden with calories. Cook simple dishes; people hopefully visit you to enjoy your company. Many people cook elaborate meals to impress their guests, then spend most of the time in the kitchen. Concentrate on creating a friendly atmosphere rather than some exotic dish.

Recipes for special dinners – starters

Here are some recipes that are compatible with the Eating Plan. Also use your imagination and follow your favourite recipes, adapting them by making the relevant substitutions.

SMOKED SALMON MOUSSE
This is not as expensive a dish as it sounds, because you can often

buy off-cuts of smoked salmon from a delicatessen at a very reasonable price.

175g (6oz) smoked salmon off-cuts
350g (12oz) low fat cream cheese
2 tbsp yogurt, chilled
Freshly ground black pepper
Cayenne pepper

Serves 6

Cut up the smoked salmon and put into blender bowl, together with the cream cheese and yogurt. Blend for a few seconds to make a creamy paste and season to taste. Divide the mousse between six little dishes and garnish each with a sprinkling of cayenne pepper.
  Serve with hot wholemeal toast or crispbread.

PRAWNS IN GARLIC BUTTER
75g (3oz) butter
1 small onion
2 large cloves of garlic
350g (12oz) prawns
1 tbsp chopped parsley
Salt and freshly ground black pepper
1 lemon
Cayenne pepper

Serves 4

Melt the butter in a frying pan. Peel and slice the onion thinly and peel and crush the garlic. Fry gently in the butter for about 4 minutes. Add the prawns and shake the pan to coat them well with the garlic butter. Cook for a further 4 minutes.
  Stir in the parsley and season with a little salt and black pepper and the cayenne pepper to taste. Place on a heated serving dish and serve hot with a wedge of lemon and wholemeal bread.

MACKEREL PÂTÉ
4 smoked mackerel fillets
1 lemon, juice and grated rind
100g (3½oz) low fat cream cheese
225g (8oz) butter, melted

Salt
Freshly ground black pepper
25g (1oz) stuffed green olives

Serves 4

Skin and flake the mackerel fillets. Place half the fillets in a blender with half of the lemon juice and rind, half of the cream cheese and melted butter. Blend until the pâté is smooth. Season to taste. Repeat with the remaining mackerel fillets and the rest of the ingredients. Pour the mixture into a small casserole and smooth the top. Slice the olives and use to decorate the top of the pâté.

Serve with slices of hot wholemeal toast or crispbreads.

Main courses

VENISON IN THE PINK

(Taken from *The New Cookbook* by Miriam Polunin)

450g (1lb) venison, cut into 4 pieces
120ml (4fl oz) port
120ml (4fl oz) red wine vinegar
120ml (4fl oz) water
1 tbsp oil
1 onion, sliced
1 raw beetroot, cut in chunks
3 to 4 stalks celery, roughly chopped
1 carrot, roughly chopped
10 juniper berries
4 black peppercorns
1 sprig of fresh rosemary or ½ tsp dried rosemary
Crumbled bay leaf

Serves 4

Place the venison in a flat dish and pour over it the port, wine vinegar and water. Leave in the refrigerator for 24–48 hours. Drain, reserving the marinade.

Heat half of the oil in a large saucepan or casserole set over a high heat. Add the meat and brown it briefly, then remove it from the pan. Reduce the heat to very low. Add the onion to the pan, cover it and cook for 5 minutes.

Add the remaining oil, then the beetroot, celery and carrot and cover the pan tightly. Cook over the lowest heat for about 8–10 minutes. Add all the spices and herbs to the pan, stir, then return the browned meat to the pan.

Pour over the reserved marinade, plus extra stock, water or wine, if necessary, to cover the meat and vegetables completely (how much you need will depend largely on the size and shape of the pan or casserole).

Bring to simmering point, then cook over a low heat for at least 1½ hours, although older meat may take up to an hour longer. Luckily venison does not break up or spoil with long cooking, provided it is well covered with liquid. Check the seasoning. Remove the bay leaf before serving.

CHICKEN TERRINE

(Taken from *The New Cookbook* by Miriam Polunin)

This is a wonderful recipe. It looks and tastes superb. It is also very complicated and, unless you really love cooking, it should be kept until your eating is really under control.

350g (12oz) chicken, boned and chopped
2 egg whites
2 tbsp lemon juice
50g (2oz) shelled shrimps or prawns, finely chopped
100g (4oz) low fat soft cheese
120ml (4fl oz) smetana or thick plain low fat yogurt or soured cream
1 tsp ground coriander
½ tsp white pepper
Large pinch of sea salt
1 tbsp whisky or wine (optional)
About 8 large spinach leaves to line the terrine
1 large carrot
1 large or 2 small courgettes
1 red pepper

Serves 4–5 as a main course or 6–7 as a starter

Place the chicken, egg whites and lemon juice in a blender or food processor and blend them to a smooth paste. Stir in the shrimps or prawns, then the cheese, smetana, coriander, seasoning and whisky. Chill the paste while you prepare the terrine dish.

Dip the spinach leaves in boiling water for about 40 seconds, then drain them. Grease a terrine dish or 1kg (2lb) loaf tin and line it with some of the leaves, holding back enough leaves to cover the top.

Chop the carrot, courgette and pepper in long, very thin pieces. Cook each vegetable in a separate saucepan in a little water, allowing 5 minutes for the carrots and 3 minutes each for the others. Drain, keeping the water for your stock jug.

Put the quarter of the chicken mixture in the dish, smoothing it down to make a thin layer. Then tap the dish firmly a few times on a wooden board to shake the mixture down well and eliminate air pockets. Make a single layer of the carrot strips on top of the chicken mixture. Add another quarter of the chicken mixture, then a layer of the courgette strips, then chicken, then the pepper strips, then the remaining chicken. Heat the oven to 300°F/150°C, gas mark 2. Boil a kettle.

Fold the retained spinach over the top of the mixture and cover with kitchen foil. Put the dish in a roasting tin and pour in boiling water from the kettle to half-fill the tin. Bake the terrine for about 45 minutes. To check that it's cooked, peel back a corner of foil and leaf: the chicken mixture should be firm and white. Chill the terrine for at least 5 hours.

To turn it out, invert a serving dish over the terrine dish, and, holding the two dishes firmly together, turn the terrine dish upside down. A firm tap should dislodge the terrine.

Using a very sharp serrated knife, cut 2cm (¾in) thick slices, holding each slice upright with a broad spatula until you have finished cutting it.

GRILLED RED MULLET WITH FENNEL

(Taken from *The 60-Minute Cookbook* by Pamela Westland)

About 1¼kg (3lb) red mullet or sea bass, cleaned
  (you can cook either large or small fish in this way)
Handful of dried fennel stalks
Olive oil
Salt
Freshly ground black pepper
About 4 tbsp brandy

Serves 6

Line the rack of the grill pan with foil and criss-cross some dried fennel stalks over it. Pre-heat the grill to hot.

Slash the fish with a sharp knife twice on each side. Brush the fish liberally with olive oil on both sides and season well with salt and pepper. Turn the grill down to moderate. Grill the fish until it is crisp and golden brown, turn it over and grill the other side. The time will of course depend on the size and thickness of the fish – a total time of about 15–24 minutes. Test with a sharp knife to make sure the fish is cooked. If any red juices run, brush with more oil and continue cooking.

Put the brandy in a small pan and heat it while the fish is cooking.

Transfer the fennel stalks to make a bed on a heated serving dish and lay the fish on top. Pour on the heated brandy and set light to it. Bring the dish to the table at once, the flames leaping and the fennel charring.

ORANGE CHICKEN
6 chicken joints
2 medium-sized onions
1 large clove of garlic
2 oranges
2 tbsp vegetable oil
2 tsp turmeric
750ml (1¼pt) chicken stock or stock cubes
1 tbsp lemon juice
Salt
Freshly ground black pepper
Pinch of ground coriander
Sachet of sweetener
2 tsp cornflour (2 tsp of cornflour divided between 6 people is not
    going to do any damage!)

Serves 6

Skin the chicken joints and prick the flesh all over with a large needle. Peel and slice the onions, and peel and crush the garlic. Slice the oranges. Heat the vegetable oil in a large frying pan and fry the onions and garlic for 3–4 minutes.

Add the chicken joints and fry for about 10 minutes, turning and browning the meat on each side. Stir in the turmeric and slowly pour over the chicken stock and lemon juice. Bring the sauce to the boil and season with salt, pepper, a pinch of coriander and the sweetener. Add the orange slices, cover the pan and simmer over a low heat for about 15 minutes.

Blend the cornflour with a little water to make a smooth paste. Pour over the chicken, stirring, and increase the heat to bring the sauce back to the boil. Boil for 2 minutes. Place the chicken pieces on a heated serving dish and pour the sauce over them.

MARINATED HALIBUT STEAKS
2 225g (9oz) halibut steaks

For the marinade
5 tbsp vegetable oil
5 tbsp tarragon vinegar
2 bay leaves
2 tbsp chopped parsley
¼ level tsp dried tarragon
1 tsp Worcestershire sauce
2 level tsp salt
¼ tsp pepper
Chopped parsley

Serves 4

Place the fish in a large shallow dish in a single layer. Combine the oil and vinegar and add the herbs, Worcestershire sauce and seasonings and stir well. Pour the mixture over the fish, turning them to cover well on both sides. Place foil over the dish and refrigerate for about 3 hours, turning the fish occasionally.

Drain the fish before grilling it for about 15 minutes or until it is tender, basting regularly with the marinade (test with a fork and if the flesh flakes easily then it is cooked).

Garnish with chopped parsley just before serving.

TARRAGON FISH
750g (1½lb) white fish fillets
4 tbsp vegetable oil
1 tbsp lemon juice
½ tsp dried tarragon or 1½ tsp chopped fresh tarragon

½ tsp salt
Pinch of pepper
Lemon slices
Chopped parsley or sprigs of parsley

Serves 4

Combine the oil, lemon juice, tarragon, salt and pepper in a small bowl. Place the fish in the grill pan and pour the tarragon mixture over the fillets, coating both sides. Grill under a high heat for between 5–8 minutes, or until the fish flakes easily when tested with a fork.

Place the fillets on a serving plate and garnish with lemon slices and parsley.

Desserts

Choose either fresh fruit, a cheeseboard or any of the recipes given in chapter six.

Celebrations – children's parties

One idea for children's parties is to substitute the traditional sandwiches with something more imaginative such as baked potatoes stuffed with a variety of fillings like grated cheese, sugar-free baked beans, chilli con carne (made to your own recipe), scrambled egg, chicken or ham in soured cream, Fromage Blanc, sweetcorn on its own or with ham or chicken, chicken in mayonnaise, prawns in cottage cheese, or anything else that takes your fancy. Or you could serve home-made meat balls on cocktail sticks, or chicken legs, or home-made beef-burgers and wholemeal rolls. Also see chapter ten for some recipes for meat loaves, which are excellent for children's parties. Then for the 'sweet' part, choose any of the desserts from chapter six, or adapt one of your own recipes so that it fits in with the Eating Plan.

'It's my birthday.'

There is no reason why you should do the cooking on your birthday, so ask your husband to give you a break or if your children are old enough, get them to help too. If you do cook for the family without their help you may feel resentful and end up bingeing. Don't put the emphasis for your celebration on a meal. Ask to be treated to the theatre or cinema instead.

At children's birthday parties take them swimming, to the park or the beach, rather than spend half the day preparing lots of jellies, sandwiches, cakes and plates of biscuits that you know will be hard to resist.

It is up to you whether you refuse or accept a slice of birthday cake. Remember that one slice can trigger a binge. It is better to be firm with yourself and try to lose your sweet-tooth permanently rather than constantly fight against temptation.

'It's Christmas.'

Christmas is the hardest time of the year for compulsive eaters. There is an abundance of food around making it difficult to resist tucking into mince pies and Christmas pudding along with everyone else. Some people give up the battle and use Christmas as an excuse for a mammoth binge, promising themselves they will start the Eating Plan on January 1. Christmas comes every year, and so does the opportunity to make – and break – New Year resolutions. It is far better to get your eating under control before Christmas so you can enjoy the celebrations and not fear bingeing.

For compulsive eaters who are lonely, it is a time when they feel at their lowest and turn to food for comfort. Try to solve your loneliness and you will be on your way to solving your eating problem. Pair up with someone else who lives alone at Christmas or volunteer to help with the Christmas Day celebrations organised for the elderly or under-privileged children. These groups always welcome a willing pair of hands.

You don't have to stick to the traditional Christmas Fare. Why not try something different to turkey and all the trimmings. Or you could keep the turkey and scrap the pies and puddings; they are not necessities and send most of the family to sleep all afternoon anyway. Try something more refreshing, such as the desserts suggested elsewhere in this book, or hot fruit salad with cream, or pineapple velvet (see p.73). The cream won't hurt you just for today.

Christmas is a time when most mothers concentrate on making everyone else happy. Put yourself first for a change. Plan ahead and work out a simpler menu so you spend less time slaving over a hot stove in the kitchen and more time having fun with your family. The children will be much happier to have you around playing with them than stuck in the kitchen getting grumpy.

A word here about stuffing for the turkey or chicken. We have noticed over the years at the Maisner Centre that compulsive eaters tend to think that stuffing is for them and not for the poultry! It appears to be a very dangerous trigger food, so if you are having trouble with your eating, it is recommended that you do not stuff your Christmas poultry. However if you feel that you can control your food, here are two delicious recipes for stuffing which are completely compatible with the Eating Plan.

If you are going to have turkey, these two following recipes which I have taken from *The Low Blood Sugar Cookbook* by Francyne Davis (Bantam Books) are excellent, as are all the recipes in this extremely useful little book.

PORK STUFFING FOR FOWL
1¼kg (2½lb) lean pork, finely ground
¼ cup parsley, chopped
1 clove of garlic, minced
1 tsp thyme
1 tsp salt
2 eggs, slightly beaten
1 tsp pepper
¼ tsp nutmeg
1 tsp sage
½ tsp chopped chives
½ tsp tabasco

Makes about 5 cups

Brown the pork in a large, heavy skillet, breaking up the meat with a fork. Remove from the heat and add the remaining ingredients. Mix well. Refrigerate until ready to use.

VEGETABLE STUFFING FOR FOWL
3 tbsp salad oil
1 onion, chopped
1 green pepper, chopped
1 large aubergine, peeled and chopped
½lb mushrooms, chopped

½ clove of garlic, minced
¼ tsp basil
¼ tsp rosemary
¼ tsp thyme
Salt to taste
Pepper to taste
1 egg, well beaten
3 tbsp soya flour

Makes about 5 cups

In a large, heavy skillet, heat the oil. Combine the onion, green pepper, aubergine, mushrooms and garlic and sauté until vegetables are tender. Add seasonings, soya flour and egg. Mix thoroughly. Remove from heat. Refrigerate until ready to use.

'I am going to a restaurant.'

There is no need to refuse an invitation to a restaurant when you are following the Eating Plan. Some restaurants serve more suitable foods than others, so get to know where they are, but there is always something on a menu that you can eat. Plan what you are going to order by knowing your best choices, such as grilled fish or baked chicken with green vegetables or salad. Remember that the restaurant is there to serve you, you are paying for the meal so ask for the food you want. Don't be worried about asking for dishes to be adapted, restaurants are used to making changes to suit customers, health or religious needs. For example, request that the vegetables are not served with butter and avoid rich sauces and dressings, if you are trying to lose weight. If there is a dish of fish in a cream sauce, ask for it to be plainly grilled and served without the sauce. If a chicken dish includes chips, ask for no chips but extra salad instead. Say 'No thank you', to the roll and butter – if it is not in front of you, you cannot eat it. Ideally choose cheese or fruit for dessert. After your meal ask for decaffeinated coffee or tea, most restaurants serve it these days. There is nothing wrong with taking a sachet of decaffeinated drink with you. Have cream in your coffee, it might be fattening but won't affect your blood sugar level.

The following are good choices when you are eating out. The

ones marked with an asterisk are fine, but are very heavy in calories, and should not be indulged in too frequently.

Consommé
Fruit juice (check that it is sugar-free)
Tomato juice
Grapefruit (check that it is fresh, not tinned in syrup)
Oysters
Smoked salmon
Artichoke
Asparagus
Melon
Corn on the cob
Parma ham with melon
Smoked trout or eel or mackerel*
Potted shrimps*
Grilled sardines (fresh)
Fresh onion soup
Prawns
Pâté*
Avocado pear*
Taramasalata with wholemeal bread*
Chicken tikka

For main courses, choose from any grilled or roast meats, grilled or baked fish and roast poultry, omelettes or kebabs. Avoid anything with a rich sauce. When it comes to dessert, opt for fresh fruit, or fruit salad – but do check whether it has sugar in it or not – or choose from the cheeseboard.

You may think you will have to make some sacrifices, yet there is no need to feel deprived during your meal. You can enjoy luxuries, such as oysters, mussels and smoked salmon, because they do not affect your blood sugar. You will not be losing out at all, and think what you are gaining – the satisfaction of getting your eating under control. So don't feel resentful when you have to refuse the creamy trifle. You cope with other choices in your life, such as deciding between a new pair of shoes or a new dress, and it is the same with your eating – you either make the right food choices, or you don't. If your enjoyment of the evening rests on eating that trifle, then you must be dining out with the wrong company.

Even in your local café you can follow the plan. You can choose anything from bacon and eggs to an omelette. If you do decide on the 'meat and two veg,' ask for yours to be served without the gravy, and if you select fried fish, don't eat the batter.

'I am eating at a friend's house.'

Do not tell your friend that you are on a diet. You are not anyway, but if you do you will only be told that you don't need to slim and one more helping of cream gâteau won't hurt. Contact your friend before the party and tell her you cannot eat certain foods, such as white flour and sugar, because of health reasons. The plan allows you to eat butter and cream because they do not affect your blood sugar level, so do not get too upset if you are served dishes which include them. Obviously eating them every day will make you fat, but this is a special occasion.

When you visit a friend, it is traditional to take a box of chocolates or a bottle of wine. Take a bunch of flowers or, even better, offer a home-made dessert from the suggestions at the end of 'I Like Puddings' chapter. It will save your hostess time, she will probably be grateful and you can eat it without any worries too.

'I am staying at a friend's house.'

Tell your hostess what you cannot eat before you arrive. Unless you actually say what you can and cannot eat, people will assume you eat anything. The Eating Plan is not a 'faddy' diet; your hostess will realise that you are only cutting out unhealthy food, including cakes and biscuits. You could take your own food with you for snacks, such as fruit and yogurt. The majority of homes keep a supply of eggs, milk and fruit in the house anyway so it will not be difficult to keep to your routine. Many people tuck into a Danish pastry mid-morning, so don't be embarrassed to open a yogurt pot instead. You will probably find your hostess will join you.

'I was forced to eat it.'

Julia said: 'My mother makes exotic desserts for family celebrations and if I dare refuse any we have a row and she says I am spoiling the party.' No one can ever force you to do anything, especially to eat food that you do not want. You always have a choice to say 'yes' or 'no'. If you had an allergy that meant your body erupted in an itchy rash every time you ate a strawberry, you would steer clear of that fruit. It is the same with the Eating Plan. You have a problem and you must solve it; in simple terms, that means you have the choice between sticking to the plan and getting well or constantly finding yourself feebly accepting every piece of cake or biscuit you are offered purely because you do not want to hurt someone else's feelings. Start standing up for yourself. And suggest your mother tries out some of the recipes at the end of 'I Like Puddings' chapter – they are exciting enough for any celebration.

14 'I like to indulge myself.'

Everyone must indulge themselves sometimes, but there are other ways of being nice to yourself than eating cream cakes. Buy yourself a bunch of flowers, take the phone off the hook and enjoy a long soak in a bubble bath, go to the hairdressers or put your feet up and read a juicy Harold Robbins novel, a Barbara Cartland romance or whatever takes your fancy.

Spoiling yourself is often associated with eating, in the same way that mothers reward children with sweets when they have been good. Although the Eating Plan allows for goodies such as cream and butter because they do not affect the blood sugar level, you must remember that they are fattening. If you do succumb to a fattening treat, you know you will only regret it afterwards, and that can lead to a vicious circle of more bingeing, more guilt and more bingeing, and so on.

We hear some bizarre tales at the Maisner Centre from clients who set out to give themselves a treat with their favourite food and end up bingeing. Samantha decided to cook fried aubergines. She tried to calculate how many calories the aubergines contained, how many calories were in the oil and how much oil would be absorbed by the aubergines in order to work out the total calorific value of the dish. Despite her attempts to stick within a certain amount of calories, she found herself so frustrated with her calculations that she went on a mammoth binge eating everything in sight. It would have been easier to have made stuffed baked aubergines and left out the oil altogether, or said to herself, that as she was only having fried aubergines just that once, to just eat a moderate portion. This only shows how calorie counting causes so many problems.

Lynn made herself a cheesecake. She weighed and measured every ingredient and worked out the calorific value. When the cheesecake was completed she tried to estimate how many calories were in a portion and resorted to using an electronic calculator. After tormenting herself for so long she ended up confused and frustrated and ate the whole lot in one go. A fresh fruit salad would have been simpler to prepare, meant less time in the kitchen and it would not have mattered how much she ate.

Many compulsive eaters feel they must 'punish' themselves to get their eating under control. Traditional diets imply you must 'suffer to slim' and as the feelings of deprivation build up, compulsive eaters resort to treating themselves to cream cakes. Don't stick to cottage cheese, grapefruit and limp lettuce all the time as you will only feel more inclined to indulge in something that is 'naughty but nice'. Be especially kind to yourself at times of stress, like changing jobs or giving up smoking. But don't comfort yourself with sweets and cakes. They won't make you feel better and if they trigger a binge you will be left feeling worse than ever.

If you must indulge yourself with food, be adventurous and try exotic fruits, like lychees or passion fruit, or have a piece of smoked salmon or some giant prawns for a change. These will not affect your blood sugar and are more mouth-watering than a plateful of cakes.

Start thinking about what you *can* eat, don't ponder on what you *cannot*. You know that if you do eat a cream cake, the chances are you will feel so guilty afterwards that your eating will suffer badly for days. The choice is always yours.

Clare sat in a restaurant and watched in agony as her boyfriend tucked into profiterolles and cream. 'I am on a diet so I could not have any. It was torture and when I got home I stuffed myself with a loaf of bread although I had just eaten a wonderful meal.'

There is no need to sit there suffering. Clare should have asked the waiter for a fresh fruit salad, strawberries and cream or cheese and biscuits.

Diana went to a dinner party and refused the dessert. While other guests indulged in the rich chocolate gâteau, she could hardly concentrate on the conversation around her. All she wanted to do was to rush to McDonalds before it closed for the night. She left the party early and bought six apple pies from the restaurant on the way home. Diana would have been helped if she had prepared something at home to look forward to, for example a fruit salad with fromage frais or a strawberry yogurt. Another alternative would have been to tell her hostess in advance she could not eat sugar, and would it be possible to have an alternative dessert, or she could have taken a dessert round herself which everybody could have enjoyed, and would have saved her hostess preparing one course.

'The tea break is the only nice thing about my job.'

Anne said: 'I hate my job and I count the minutes to the tea break. I get so miserable at work that I need to indulge in a cake to cheer myself up.' Anne should, if it was at all possible, change her job to one where she was stimulated, so she had no need to turn to food for excitement. However, in these times of unemployment it is probably easier said than done. In her tea break she should spend the time talking with her colleagues and taking in some fruit.

'The rest of the family indulge in ice cream and sweets at the cinema, why can't I?'

Because you have an eating problem, and they do not. Take some yogurt, fruit or nuts with you instead.

'I do the week's shopping with a friend and we always treat ourselves to tea in Ye Olde Cake Shop.'

If you are in need of a sit down after shopping, why not go to a sandwich or salad bar rather than a cake shop. Or invite your friend to your home and have something savoury waiting, such as cheese and fruit. If you feel you must have a 'treat' after shopping, buy yourself a bunch of flowers instead of a cake.

It is far better not to think of food as a 'treat'. Buy yourself something tangible, like a new pair of shoes, a lipstick, a scarf or a plant, whenever you feel like being nice to yourself. They will last much longer than a doughnut, and give you much more pleasure. If you don't indulge in food, you will still be indulging yourself in other ways. You will feel better, look better and get your eating under control. That's more of a tonic than a cream cake.

15 'It's boring.'

Boredom is one of the main causes of compulsive eating. Cure your boredom and you will get your eating under control again. But first ask yourself: Are you bored with eating or bored with life?

'Food is my only pleasure' is a common cry heard at the Maisner Centre. It means you cannot stop eating chocolate bars and buns. June, a young mum with a toddler, told us: 'The only thing I get excited about is food. Life is so boring. All I think about is what I am going to eat next, going out to buy it and then sitting down to eat it. I dream about food at night and work out what I shall eat the next day. I am getting fatter and fatter but it has become an obsession.'

It is not just mums stuck at home looking after the children who turn to food for excitement. Mandy is a nurse and although her job may appear to others to be demanding and fulfilling, off-duty she binges. 'I get so bored when I am not at work. I wander around the house and usually end up sitting in front of the television scoffing anything I can find in the kitchen. Everyone says I deserve my rest because of my job, but I would rather be at work because at least I cannot constantly eat there.'

There is something drastically wrong with your life if food is your only pleasure. The more bored you become the harder the struggle to make your life exciting again. Bored people look listless and are apathetic and everything they do and see becomes a bore. Food is a comfort for them, cakes and biscuits and jam sandwiches remind them of their childhood when mummy was around to wash away the tears and entertain them. Now they are grown-up, their lifestyle is their own choice. And many compulsive eaters turn to food to escape the harsh realities.

Work out what needs changing in your life and do something about it. Maybe your work is tedious and it's time you changed your job, or perhaps a relationship has become dull and it's time you changed your partner. Life should be exciting and fun at any age, whether you are 20, 40 or drawing your pension, you can still find new interests to keep yourself active and out of the kitchen. Set yourself a challenge. There must be some subject you are interested in, perhaps it is the mating habits of canaries or the migration routes of Canadian geese. Make a list of topics you would like to know more about and join your local library to learn more about them. Even if your friends think the subject you choose is boring, don't take any notice, go ahead and become an amateur expert.

Enrol for an evening class or join a local club, and we don't necessarily mean aerobics classes or a health club. Put your energies into something that is not orientated around your image. After a few weeks you may change your mind and find the subject boring, but you will not have lost anything. At least you will know the subject is not the one for you, so pick another.

If you cannot think of a gripping hobby, why not try finding out more about where you live. Many of us live in towns and cities full of places of historical interest but never visit them. Your local library will show you where to start. Tracing your family tree can be fascinating and absorbing and starts close to home. It is also a good way of meeting long-lost relatives and making friends. Clubs are springing up all over the country as people want to discover more about their roots. Who knows, you may find yourself related to the Queen!

If you are bored because you are lonely, it is company and not food that you need. Join a club or evening class and you will soon make friends. And with your new-found interests you will always have something to talk about to the new people you meet.

People are constantly saying, 'I have always wanted to learn how to knit/sew/crochet/swim/play tennis/bowls . . .' There must be some sport or pastime that you secretly yearn to master, and why not be adventurous and tackle some of the most exciting, like hang-gliding or wind-surfing.

If you are short of money, a good way to fill your time and do something practical is to make a start on next year's Christmas presents. You can begin at any time of the year, even January. Use your imagination to make cards and gifts. You will probably save yourself a fortune as well as find your task rewarding. What about making your own pot-pourri, or growing plants from your own cuttings?

'I am bored with food.'

Being a compulsive eater is extremely boring. You think about food constantly, worrying about what you can and cannot eat, counting calories, weighing yourself each day, peering in the mirror to see if you look thinner or fatter than yesterday. There is nothing more boring to people whose eating is normal to hear compulsive eaters drone on about their diet, how much they have gained or lost and what they will do when they reach their mythical 'ideal' weight. Perhaps you are more bored with being a compulsive eater than food itself. Boredom with food is due to laziness and lack of imagination. Compulsive eaters often set themselves a rigid diet, such as grapefruit, cottage cheese, crispbreads and clear soup – the same food in the same order every day. No wonder they get bored and end up bingeing on huge mounds of cream cakes and chocolate biscuits. Your diet should be varied and it can be fun. There is no need to be bored with food while following the Eating Plan, it allows for such a wide variety of food from smoked salmon to strawberries and cream. If you do still feel bored with the plan it is because you are refusing to break-out of your usual eating regime. Start being adventurous; you can make even cottage cheese interesting by adding fruit, such as chopped crisp green apples or juicy cherries.

Buy a good cookery book with lots of step-by-step illustrations to give you inspiration. If a recipe calls for ingredients forbidden in the Eating Plan, adapt them with something which is permitted, such as using artificial sweetener instead of refined sugar, wholemeal flour instead of white flour, wholemeal breadcrumbs instead of white breadcrumbs, polyunsaturated fat instead of butter and yogurt instead of sour cream or normal cream. Experiment with herbs and spices and brighten the dish with garnish to make it look more appealing.

I recently went to a cookery class which offered an excellent recipe for Curry Mayonnaise, to be served with cold chicken or turkey. The recipe was as follows:

CURRY MAYONNAISE 1

1 tbsp oil
1 small onion, chopped finely
2 tsp curry powder
4 tbsp tomato juice
4 tbsp red wine
2 tbsp apricot jam
450ml (¾pt) mayonnaise
Salt and pepper (optional)

In a saucepan heat the oil and sauté the onion until soft but not brown. Add the curry powder and cook gently for 2 minutes. Add the tomato juice and red wine and simmer until reduced by half. Stir in the apricot jam, cool and strain, pressing well to extract the liquid. Stir this mixture into the mayonnaise to make a sauce that coats the back of a spoon. If necessary, add 1 tablespoon warm water to the mayonnaise to thin it. Season to taste.

Now, I was able to take this recipe and adapt it so that it was in line with the Eating Plan, and still tasted delicious.

CURRY MAYONNAISE 2

½ chicken stock cube and 2 tbsp water
1 tbsp oil
1 small onion, chopped finely
2 tsp curry paste
1 tsp tomato purée + 4 tbsp tomato juice
2 sachets of sweetener
Small tin apricots in apple juice
1½ cups of full cream natural yogurt

In a saucepan dissolve the stock cube in the water, add the oil and cook the onion until soft. Add the curry paste and cook gently for 2 minutes. Add the tomato purée and the tomato juice and simmer until reduced by half. Add the sweetener and chopped apricots and stir into the yogurt.

Think about all the different foods that you *can* eat following the Eating Plan; do not dwell on what you cannot eat. Set yourself a challenge to find something new to eat each day and still keep to the plan. Try a new fruit or vegetable or a different way of preparing them or test varieties of ham that you have not tasted before.

Here is an example of what you could eat for a day following the Eating Plan. Does it look boring to you?

Rising	Orange juice
Breakfast	Kidneys, bacon and tomato
Snack	Taramasalata with raw vegetable crudités
Lunch	Grilled Dublin Bay prawns with a green salad and lowfat garlic dressing
Snack	Shredded chicken with bamboo shoots
Dinner	Smoked salmon followed by pheasant with Brussels sprouts and broccoli tops and fresh lychees
Snack	Brie with crispbread

16 'I'm a coffee addict.'

Compulsive eaters are often heavy coffee drinkers; they say it 'peps' them up and kills their appetite, and they often object to giving it up. In fact, coffee contains caffeine which is a drug, and people who find it hard to stop drinking coffee are probably addicted to it. You should certainly kick the habit until your eating is under control, but preferably cut out coffee from your diet permanently. This might not be as difficult as you imagine, just wait and see how much better your eating is and how much healthier you feel after a few coffee-free weeks.

'Coffee is harmless.'

That seemingly harmless cup of coffee contains enough caffeine to disturb your blood sugar level and, as it reacts in your body in a similar way to sugar, it makes you hungry too. It also causes headaches, stress and anxiety – just what you don't need when you are trying to get your eating under control. Caffeine has been linked to birth defects, digestive disorders, heart disease, breast disease and anxiety attacks. It affects the central nervous system, which creates a 'hyper' feeling, which is why it is taken as a stimulant to keep sleep at bay.

We had serious doubts about whether or not we could help Ellen when she first came to the Maisner Centre. Her medical background made her appear to be unstable and perhaps a case for more qualified help than ours. However, she was so desperate and keen to do something about her eating problem that we decided that she had nothing to lose. Ellen, 45, had suffered from blinding headaches since her teens, which kept her away from school frequently and, as she reached her forties, kept her bed-bound most of the time. She was taking a great deal of medication, she was seeing a psychiatrist and had recently had a brain scan.

A week after starting on the Eating Plan she wrote:

> When I came to see you I was on the brink of suicide. But miracles do happen. Within a week of starting the Eating Plan my headaches had got so much better I was able to think about going back to work. At the end of a month I had stopped all medication, found a job and was picking up my career again. Coffee must be the cause of the headaches. On the few occasions that I have had a cup since, I have immediately had a blinding headache. I will never again touch coffee.

Ellen's eating is now under control too.

'Coffee makes me slim.'

Caffeine raises the body's metabolic rate, increasing the number of calories your body burns. You may think that will help you lose weight, but before you reach for the coffee jar, remember that at the same time caffeine triggers the release of insulin which in turn causes your blood sugar level to drop, and before long you are feeling hungry. Caffeine also destroys some of the vitamin B complex and acts as a diuretic making you lose vital nutrients.

'I cannot stop drinking coffee.'

Many compulsive eaters become coffee addicts after following weight-loss diets which recommend a daily dosage of coffee. But as little as three or four cups a day can make you physically and psychologically addicted to caffeine.

If you are a heavy coffee drinker, breaking the habit can lead to some unpleasant withdrawal symptoms, such as headaches, lethargy, depression and irritability. There are two ways to tackle your addiction. You can go 'cold turkey' and cut it out completely, which may mean you face the withdrawal symptoms and can feel ill for about four days. It may be better to cut down gradually by blending your normal brand of coffee with decaffeinated coffee. Most shops sell decaffeinated brands and although it is sometimes a little more expensive, it is worth it as you will quickly feel the benefits.

Tea contains caffeine, too, but not in such high quantities as coffee. Weak tea is not too harmful, but try herbal teas that do not contain caffeine.

Many soft drinks, including low-calorie brands, also contain caffeine, so check the label before you buy. Caffeine is also found in chocolate and even pain-killing tablets, so be sure to avoid brands that contain it.

'Coffee stops me eating.'

Many people do believe that coffee curbs their appetite, because it is included in so many weight-loss diets. Caffeine creates only a temporary halt to your appetite, before long you will be feeling hungry and also stressed, perfect conditions for a binge.

'Everyone I know drinks coffee.'

That is no reason why you should drink it too. You have an eating problem and if you want to get back to normal eating you must be prepared to make changes. If friends visit, offer them decaffeinated coffee, it looks and tastes the same as caffeinated brands, but has none of the harmful side-effects. They will not know they are drinking decaffeinated coffee unless you tell them. Many herbal teas are also decaffeinated and much more refreshing than a cup of coffee. Your friends may be delighted to try something different for a change.

'My friends don't have decaffeinated coffee.'

If this is the case, ask for tea instead when you visit your friends. Good friends will not object if you take your own decaffeinated coffee with you, especially if you explain to them how much healthier decaffeinated coffee is. You may well persuade them to give it a try too.

'I like to drink coffee after a meal in a restaurant.'

Many cafés and restaurants serve decaffeinated coffee these days. Simply ask the waiter. If they do not serve it, stick to tea instead or take a sachet of your own coffee with you.

Caffeine affects people in different ways. Some suffer from blinding headaches or get the 'shakes' after just one cup of coffee. After getting her eating under control, Vera said: 'I feel sure that the main cause of my problem was coffee. Since cutting out caffeine I feel immeasurably better, I have not had violent swings of mood or cravings for food.'

I gave up coffee for four years and now drink it rarely. If I do not drink it too frequently I am fine, but as soon as I have a few cups of coffee in one day I get very tired and irritable. I went back to drinking large quantities of black coffee late at night when I first started working on this book. I soon found I wanted more and more and I was getting tired and jittery. I started to eat more and I put on weight. Some people never learn, do they? However, I spoke sternly to myself and followed my own advice and was surprised how easily I gave up coffee *and* how much better I felt for it.

Your body may be able to cope with caffeine, once your eating is under control again. Test yourself carefully by drinking one cup. If you feel the slightest effect afterwards, then you know that caffeine is not for you and you should continue to avoid it.

17 'I don't want to give up alcohol.'

Alcohol is fattening, lowers your blood sugar level, weakens your will-power and acts as a depressant. You must give up drink at least temporarily if you want to get your eating under control. There are no exceptions to this rule.

Yet this is probably the one aspect of the Eating Plan which many people object to most of all. It is surprising how many find it difficult to give up alcohol, even only for a month, until their eating is under control. We are not teetotallers, we believe that for many people there is nothing wrong with enjoying a celebratory drink or wine with a meal – once your eating is under control.

Sheena spent seventeen years seeking treatment for compulsive eating and bulimia from doctors and psychiatrists. She claimed she did not have a drink problem, but each day she had a sherry at noon and wine with her lunch and evening meal. As soon as she started the Eating Plan she got her eating under control. But a few months later at a Christmas party she accepted a few drinks. 'I binged until I was sick. I will never drink again. I now know I am one of those people who cannot tolerate a drink. I accept this is a very low price for having my eating under control.'

Even if you do only occasionally have a drink, don't think that won't count. You probably will not miss alcohol, but those who drink even just a couple of times a week may find it harder. You must cut out alcohol completely, don't tell yourself that 'Just one little one won't hurt.' So many people treat themselves to a tipple in the evening and do not binge – yet gorge themselves the next day. Until they stop drinking, they won't stop bingeing.

Alcohol is extremely high in calories, and these are empty calories containing no nutrients. People who drink a lot tend to eat poorly. The more they drink the less attention they are likely to pay to what they eat. If they are following a calorie-controlled diet, which we do not recommend, they can easily use up much of their daily ration of calories on alcohol.

In small doses alcohol is generally an appetite stimulant, but larger amounts can suppress hunger in some cases. This won't help your eating problem. Even if alcohol prevents you bingeing temporarily, once the effects have worn off you will binge.

As well as the toxic effects of alcohol on the liver, drink also deprives the body of nutrients from the food that is eaten. Alcohol uses up vital vitamins and because it is a diuretic it increases the output of urine and causes the loss of minerals. It also does nothing for your appearance, people who drink a lot often have bloodshot eyes and a puffy face.

Women are generally more sensitive to alcohol than men. Researchers believe this is because men have a higher percentage of water in their bodies, so the alcohol becomes more diluted. It is believed that women who drink immediately prior to a period get drunk easier than at other times of the month.

However much you may enjoy a drink, the 'morning after' is nothing to look forward to. Even if you do not have a hangover, you won't feel on form. Hangovers can make you vomit, and feel tired and depressed. It will be much easier to get your eating under control when you are not faced with coping with these feelings.

Marie got her eating under control by following the Eating Plan, but a year later she contacted the Centre to say she needed help again. She had four children, including a small baby, and her husband had started to work overtime at the weekends. She said:

'I find the weekends hardest to take, with nothing to look forward to but cooking and cleaning and looking after the children. So I always buy myself a bottle of whisky. I know it makes me feel guilty and depressed, and it always makes me binge afterwards, but I find myself looking forward to when I can drink myself into a stupor, and not think of anything else for a few hours.'

The solution to Marie's problems does not lie in alcohol, which is only making her binge again, but in re-arranging her life.

'I cannot give up alcohol.'

Remember that it is only a temporary ban, and if you cannot give up alcohol for a month or so until your eating is under control, then you probably have a drink problem as well as an eating problem. As well as needing advice with your eating you should seek professional help to combat your drinking. Contact your GP or your local branch of Alcoholics Anonymous (their number will be in the telephone directory).

We are not asking you to attempt an impossible feat. Take it one day at a time. You may find it tough at first so start thinking of all the positive reasons why you should give up drink, such as saving money, reducing the risk of bingeing, looking better and feeling in control of yourself. Next time you drink too much, take a good look at yourself and how you are behaving, for drink brings out the worst in people. When you weigh up the pros and cons you should not feel that you are missing out on anything by staying sober.

'I have to drink with my husband because he does not like to drink alone and I do not want to spoil his pleasure.'

Stop using your husband as an excuse for your own problem. If you truly want to stop drinking, start putting yourself first. Would you take heroin if he was an heroin addict? Of course you would not. Explain to him that you must not drink until your eating is under control. Surely he would prefer you to get your eating under control and be happy, rather than drink and binge. If he does not understand then he must be a selfish man, making himself happy while causing you distress. He may be using your company to ease his own guilt for drinking. You can always refuse to drink with him or share his company. If you cannot make him understand, then make sure you pour out the drinks. Give him a vodka and orange juice and pour a straight juice for yourself. He will never know the difference.

'All my friends drink.'

Are all your friends compulsive eaters? The answer is probably 'NO', so start realising that you have a problem that needs tackling. They don't. If you are concerned what they will think of you and whether you will feel left out if you do not drink, then perhaps it is time to change your friends. Find somebody who will stimulate your mind and then you will not miss alcohol.

I now realise that when I had an eating problem I was mixing with people who drank excessively. These days my eating is under control and I do not have any friends who drink, except, like me, on special occasions.

'People force me to drink.'

Do they tie you down and pour drink down your throat? No one forces you to do anything, you always have a choice. Do not mix with people who bully you into drinking. Real friends respect your wishes.

'I have no self-confidence unless I drink.'

Self-confidence produced by drink is a false confidence. You are avoiding reality. Most people are boring and tiresome when they drink, you are probably the same so there is no reason to feel confident when you are drinking. If you must have something in your hand in a pub, hold a glass of mineral water, or fresh fruit juice.

'I have a reputation for drinking.'

Are you proud of it? Change your image.

'It helps me to relax.'

Discover what is making you tense, and solve that. There are other ways of relaxing that do truly work and will not cause you to binge. Take up exercise, yoga or meditation.

'It helps me to sleep.'

Try to solve your worries and problems, don't drown them in drink. You know your problems won't disappear overnight and the more you drink the less capable you will be of thinking straight and working out a solution. If you find it difficult to sleep, it may help to take up exercise to relax you, or go to bed later and take a book with you. One of the best ways to get a night's sleep is to use a Maisner Method cassette.

'It makes me feel better.'

At the time it might, but do the after-effects make you feel good too? If you need alcohol to make you feel good you must start facing up to what is making you feel bad in the first place. Your problem won't go away because you have a couple of drinks. Start solving the cause of the drinking, it is probably your eating anyway. Research shows that it is nonsense to say that alcohol makes you feel good. Alcohol is a depressant, it may give you an initial lift, but it soon lets you down with a bump.

'It's Christmas and everyone else is drinking.'

Christmas is the most difficult time of the year to keep your eating under control because of the abundance of food. When you drink your will-power is lowered and your blood sugar level drops, which makes it harder for you to resist temptation. Alcohol affects everyone, not just compulsive eaters. At Christmas most people drink more and at the same time they eat more too. Ask yourself what you would rather have, a drink and a binge or no drink and a happy Christmas? Volunteer to be the only sober one to drive everyone else home if you need an added incentive to keep off alcohol at parties. It will make you popular too.

'I always drink when I'm alone in the house.'

This is the worst reason for drinking. You must start to change your lifestyle; whenever you feel like a drink get out of the house, go for a walk, visit friends or go to the cinema. If you live alone there is no reason for you to keep alcohol in the house. Peggy always kept a few bottles. 'But not for myself', she said, 'just to give to other people when they visited.' But, of course, when she was alone she drank them herself.

Lorraine drank all day each Sunday to stop herself eating and went to bed with a sleeping pill. 'I had a whole day once a week without bingeing and without thinking of food because I was so drunk.' She woke every Monday morning and binged. Lorraine had cut out one day of her life each week. She had to completely re-think her life and find herself better things to do on Sundays before she solved her eating problem.

'My hobby is wine-making.'

Give all the bottles away and change your hobby.

'All my friends get drunk on Saturday night.'

Go out with them and stay sober. They might seem fun when you are drunk too, but in the cold light of day you will probably find them boring and will want to find some new friends.

'I cannot make love when I'm sober.'

You must be going to bed with the wrong man for the wrong reasons. You need to improve your confidence and your image of yourself. Talk to your doctor or seek advice from the Marriage Guidance Council, they help single people too (their number will be in your telephone directory).

Make yourself a set of rules if you want to return to drinking after your eating is under control. For example: never drink alone; always eat before you drink – remember that alcohol affects your blood sugar so line your stomach with some protein so the alcohol will not have such a traumatic effect on you, something quick and simple, like a glass of milk or a yogurt, will help; avoid sweet drinks, like sherry and liqueurs and also aperitifs, which are appetite stimulants; discover by trial and error if you can drink again, and if so, what drink will not make you binge.

A number of recipes in this book contain alcohol. It will do you no harm to eat these dishes as the alcohol is evaporated in the cooking, leaving just the taste. Avoid them if you know you will be tempted to finish off the bottle while cooking.

18 'It's more difficult for women

Compulsive eating is considered a 'women's problem', yet far more men suffer than most people realise. However, while overweight men are thought of as enjoying a good appetite and being macho, women are under intense pressure to be slim. We believe that as many as one woman in four suffers at some time from an eating problem.

The media is mainly to blame. Advertisements everywhere, in buses, trains, magazines, newspapers and television, portray the 'ideal' woman. She is tall, slim and glamorous. And even in these liberated times women lacking in self-confidence believe the media message that being slim means being loved and successful. They forget that for the models their looks are their lives, and most of them have to work hard at exercise and diet every day. In the same way that a cabbie cares for his taxi, models must care for their bodies. If they slip up, they won't get work. How they look is a full-time job for most models.

But women face a challenge every day. Food is the centre of the family life. They have to plan meals, go shopping, cook for the children and then for their husbands. Housewives stuck at home all day have easy access to the enemy – the fridge.

Many compulsive eaters suffer from marriage and relationship problems, which they struggle to combat alongside their eating disorder. They turn to food at moments of stress, perhaps they feel bored or resentful at being hemmed in by marriage, or they may not be able to cope with caring for their husbands, children and fulfilling their career ambitions.

The traditional role of women is changing. Women now have an alternative to getting married, motherhood and living their lives through their husbands. The role of a housewife is said to be unfulfilling to many women, but this has caused confusion and feelings of inadequacy among women who do want that lifestyle. Those women who choose a career face constant pressure to succeed in what is often a male-orientated world while harbouring feelings of guilt for neglecting their husbands and children. Lack of self-confidence at home or at work can make compulsive eaters turn to food for comfort.

Women have always been the carers in society. They cook, clean and look after their families. They listen to the problems of neighbours and friends, yet some women cannot find anyone to talk to themselves when they need a shoulder to lean on. They bottle up their emotions and eat to release the feelings of loneliness and despair.

Many compulsive eaters do not like themselves, they feel fat and ugly and hate their fear and addiction to food. They mistakenly believe that by always saying 'yes' to everyone else's needs, they will be liked. Feeling trodden on and neglected makes a compulsive eater substitute food for love.

Sarah weighed 16 stone and felt that life was not worth living. Whenever she tried to explain her problem to her family she was told not to be 'stupid' and they continued to insist that she cooked proper meals, that meant chips with everything and treacle pudding to follow. They protested when she sat at the table with them with a salad or fish dish. To keep the peace she gave in.

She said: 'I am to blame. I thought it would make my husband happy and that he would love me if I did what he wanted all the time. It is my fault. I should have kept my own identity. I should not have allowed myself to become a slave.'

Women turn themselves into the family waitress, maid, washer-up and general dogsbody voluntarily. You always have a choice over your actions. You owe it to yourself to change your life in order to get your eating under control. The longer you allow your family to walk right over you, the harder it will be to stop, and meanwhile you will continue to feel resentful, miserable and turn to food for solace. Start thinking about yourself, do what you want when you want, and do not feel guilty. You are not just a 'mother', or a 'wife', but a PERSON, with equal rights to be cared for and given support by the rest of the family. In fact, you will soon find that your family respects you more for standing up for yourself.

Jane's husband telephoned the Maisner Centre demanding to know what we had done to his wife. He said: 'She has changed her personality. She is telling me what she wants to do. She has chosen the colour of the new living room curtains!' Jane had also got her eating under control.

Get to know yourself instead of living your life through the needs of others, your husband and your children. You deserve to spend some time on yourself, even if it is only 30 minutes a day. Ask your partner to take his turn to look after the children, even if he allows you just enough time for a long, leisurely, peaceful bath. Take the children to a playgroup if they are young, or find another mother and take turns looking after her children for an afternoon a week. If the children are at school, do not spend the day cleaning, shopping and cooking. Leave out one chore and set aside an hour for you, read a book, go for a walk in the park, write letters or better still take up a new hobby or interest. You will discover a new you and your family will appreciate you more.

'My husband does not understand my eating problem.'

It may seem an impossible task, but do try to talk to your husband. He may already be aware, or at least suspect, that there is something wrong. Whether he ever discovers you bingeing or you hide yourself in the toilet or wait until he is out of the house, the cost of your addiction is hard to keep secret.

It is difficult to explain to others, even your partner, what being a compulsive eater means. He may think you are greedy or lacking in will-power. He could be more understanding if you said you were addicted to drugs rather than food. Explain to him that it is an illness, but not the same as chicken-pox or a cold. It will not simply go away by itself.

It will be a great relief for you to get your problem out in the open; even if he is not entirely sympathetic at first, at least you are no longer keeping it a secret from him. For his part, he can now see a reason for your behaviour and changes in mood.

If he will not listen at first, do not give up. Make him understand that you need his support if you are to gain the confidence to get well again, and when that happens your relationship with him should improve too. You will feel happier and full of energy when your eating is under control.

'My husband will not allow me to eat salads.'

Mandy said: 'My husband goes mad every time he sees "rabbit" food in the house. He likes fry-ups and chips with everything and he insists I eat the same as him. We have a row every time I try to make a salad, even if it is just for me.'

Married compulsive eaters often use their husbands as an excuse for their own lack of self-assertion. What sort of ogre did you marry? Stop being so feeble, stand up for yourself. Insist that you want to eat salads, they are healthier for you and him, but if he still wants his fry-ups, cook his meal separately to keep him happy. What is the worst effect your action will bring? You may have a row, but instead of backing down as usual, stick to your guns. Tell him you still love and respect him, but he is no longer going to control what you eat.

It may seem hard to start making changes, especially if you are lacking in confidence. Friends and family may be surprised at first when you start insisting on doing what you want to do for a change, do not let it worry you. You must not be afraid to be different from everyone else in order to get your eating back to normal.

'I hate cooking.'

Many women, even in today's liberated world, are raised to believe that cooking is a 'woman's task'. Cooking for their families is supposed to be an act of love, and they should cheerfully and willingly be busy in the kitchen. If women hate cooking they feel guilty. Others resent cooking, slaving over a hot stove they feel like the family servant and their frustration and resentment grows. Many compulsive eaters also hate cooking because they fear food. Working in the kitchen for a time is too much of a temptation and they begin to dread mealtimes.

Be honest, start admitting to your friends and family that you hate cooking and you will find you are not alone. Do not feel guilty, or resentful, start solving the problem. There are other ways to show your love, through affection, talking and spending time with your children and husband. Have you told your husband that you loathe cooking? Often men do not share the cooking because they believe their wife does not want them in the kitchen, or they feel shy about having a go in case they make a mistake. Ask your partner, he may be yearning to cook for you. Even if he is not too keen on the idea get him to take turns with you. Encourage your children to help too, there may be a few burnt offerings to start with, but do not put them off, they may turn out to be wonderful willing cooks.

There is no need to spend a lot of time in the kitchen if you hate cooking. You can prepare all sorts of meals for all occasions quickly. Learn how to cut corners. Use frozen food and vegetables, there is nothing unhealthy about them. Tinned food is also handy, check the label first and only buy products without any added sugar. Keep ready-made processed meals for emergencies. Again check the ingredients, there are now many brands on the market that do not contain additives and sugar. Keep a store of foods that can be quickly turned into healthy meals, such as tins of tuna which can be used in a salad or served hot baked with vegetables. Buy a slow cooker to save you hours preparing a meal. It takes 10 minutes to put together a casserole, simply add chopped carrots, potatoes, celery and a tin of tomatoes and a stock cube to a couple of joints of chicken. You do not need to think about the meal until the dish is ready to serve for dinner. Invest in a microwave, it takes no time for a meal to be cooked, even straight from the freezer.

Concentrate on what you do best in the kitchen, there must be some aspect of cooking that you hate the least. Try not to let yourself get bored with your food choices, as boredom with food can often lead to bingeing. Experiment by adapting your favourite recipes with different vegetables, herbs and spices.

'I binge when my family will not help around the house.'

Stop blaming your family, it is your fault for not insisting they help. Washing-up and cooking are not 'women's work', and you should not feel guilty or a failure for wanting your family to help with the chores.

More husbands these days are seeing their marriage as a partnership in and out of the kitchen. If yours does not, try to get him to change with the times. If you both work, there is no reason why he should not pull his weight around the home. Even if he cannot cook, he can at least wash up. Explain to him that if he helped the jobs would be done twice as quickly so that you could spend more time together. Your message might do wonders for your love life too.

It is not easy to change family habits, but you must make the effort if you no longer want to be a 'slave' to your family. If everyone takes turns hanging out the washing, dusting or washing-up, you will find yourself feeling less resentful about doing other chores for them, because you know they do something for you too.

Do not keep the children out of the kitchen, start them helping at a young age. Make it fun to begin with and even if they can only do the simplest tasks, like laying the table or washing the lettuce, it will save you some time.

There is no reason why older children should not take turns cooking the evening meal instead of you. If they complain tell them they had better get on with it because you will not be cooking for them that evening. They will soon be busy in the kitchen, and they will probably find it fun too. It is never too late to get your family to change. Explain that running the house takes team work, it is not your job to make sure that the home is always clean and tidy, that their ironing has been done, the toothpaste has not run out and there is enough loo paper for the weekend. Get your family to take responsibility too.

'I binge when my husband goes out and I'm left alone.'

Caroline told us: 'When my husband is late home because of work or if he is out with his mates, I cannot stop eating. He is always saying he will be home at a certain time and arrives two hours later. By then I have usually eaten his meal as well as mine and anything else that is in the house.'

Instead of feeling resentful and angry when your partner is late, try to fill your time with positive activities; immerse yourself in a good book or make yourself a new skirt or knit a jumper. Keep your hands and mind occupied. Explain to your partner how you suffer when he is late. Try to get him to understand that you have an eating problem which you are finding hard to control when he is being thoughtless. You both must work out how to change your relationship if you are to overcome your problems. Perhaps you should go out together more. Don't make excuses, start tackling your problems without delay. Just talking to your partner will clear the air and make you feel so much better.

'I binge on Sunday when the family go out and leave me to cook the dinner.'

Stop resenting your family, instead get up and join them. Serve the meal later in the afternoon so you can go out with your husband and take the children too. Your family will enjoy your company more than a big meal. If they do still want their three-course Sunday lunch with all the trimmings, tell them they will have to help or you will not bother cooking on a grand scale. Don't feel guilty about cooking smaller, simpler meals which are more convenient for you, and mean less time in the kitchen preparing the food and washing up the dirty dishes afterwards.

For many women cooking for their family is a symbol of love. Valerie's husband boasted to his friends how she always made him a cooked breakfast in bed at the weekends. It was not the food that pleased him, but the fact she was paying attention to him and trying to make him happy. But feeding your family is not the only way to show your love. There are other ways of showing you care, by talking to each other, going out together and sharing your time with them. Start putting less emphasis on food and more on showing your feelings and emotions. If you are pleased with your family, do not cook them jam roly-poly, instead go swimming together or treat them to the cinema. If you are upset or angry, instead of consoling yourself with a binge on cakes and biscuits, explain how you feel to your family. If you cannot put your feelings into words, write them down. Go for a walk to calm down or have a hot, relaxing bath. Get your anger out of your system and you will feel much better for it.

Many compulsive eaters turn to food when their families go off to work or to school and they are left at home feeling bored and lonely. Helen said: 'I walk around the supermarket with the devil in me. I tell myself I am buying cakes, biscuits and sweets for the children, but I know deep down they are all for me. Sometimes I don't even reach home before I eat them all, often I stuff myself sitting in the car in the car park.'

Try to keep busy doing other things. It is difficult to avoid temptation when you must shop each day for the family if it makes you feel bored and resentful. Work out why you feel these emotions and try to find a solution, perhaps teaming up with other mothers to go shopping or asking your husband if he will go with you at weekends or a late-night opening.

'I'm pregnant.'

There is an added incentive to get your eating under control when you are pregnant, for the baby's sake as well as your own. Do not start eating for two, you will only get fat. Stick to the Eating Plan and you and your baby will be getting the right vitamins and nutrients to keep healthy. Expect to gain up to 2 stone during pregnancy and it is no time to go on a diet. Yet extra weight is more difficult to lose after the birth, so start getting your eating under control before the baby arrives.

'But my baby only likes sweet foods.'

It is possible to bring up your children without giving them sugary food that can make them fat and rot their teeth. Never add sugar to baby food, even if it tastes dull to you. Tastes are acquired, babies are not born with a sweet-tooth. There are many baby foods on the market that do not contain sugar. As your child grows, never use food as a comfort or a treat and don't make a fuss about meal times. A child soon realises that food time can also be play time. Don't cook special meals for children, give your child the same food as you eat and don't put too much on his plate. If he doesn't eat it all, you will only be tempted to clean the plate yourself. If he is still hungry after a meal, give him fruit or a piece of cheese instead of sugary desserts.

Many compulsive eaters become resentful because they feel they have lost their independence by becoming a wife and mother. Others feel guilty when they are faced with the choice between making the most of their opportunities and talents and succeeding in a stimulating job, or fulfilling their natural maternal and nesting instincts. And they all feel the pressure from the media who depict women as glamorous creatures with model-girl figures while they are devoting their time and energy to cleaning the house, doing the washing and looking after the children.

You will not lose your independence at any time in your life, if you are your own person. You are responsible for your own thoughts and actions, and nothing and no one can change that. Never allow yourself to believe that you live your life only through other people, your husband and your children. You can still retain your hobbies, interests and ensure you have some time to yourself if you give the time and effort to organise your life. Whether you stay at home with a brood of kids or remain single and devote your energy to your work, it is your choice how you live.

Being a woman should not be considered a misfortune and an excuse for your eating problems. Think about the special gifts you do have as a woman, being sensitive to others' feelings and making loyal and lasting friendships with other women, the joys that come with motherhood and the fact you can openly show your emotions.

Thousands of women have followed the Eating Plan, overcome the obstacles and conquered their eating problem. Being a woman is no excuse, there is nothing you can do to change it, so start enjoying life.

'I don't like cooking.'

If you don't like to cook and you are entertaining, it is a good idea to start off with a very simple first course, such as soup, which has been made previously and frozen, and then all you have to do is to heat it up before your guests arrive; or something like avocado vinaigrette, slices of papaya sprinkled with lime juice, melon or grapefruit. Your last course, again, should be very simple, perhaps fresh fruit salad, a cheeseboard or one of the simpler desserts from Chapter Six. This only leaves you the main course and I have included some suggestions for this below. I personally have found that the best dinner parties that I have given have been cold joints of beef and turkey and cold fish, such as salmon, with numerous salads to which people can help themselves (see Chapter Five) with the dressings served separately. Served with baked potatoes, this makes an excellent buffet dinner.

Easy soups for entertaining

GAZPACHO
6 ripe tomatoes, peeled and chopped
1 small onion, chopped
½ green pepper, chopped
50g (2oz) cucumber, chopped
50g (2oz) lemon juice
8–10 drops tabasco sauce
Ice cubes

Serves 4

Place all the ingredients in a liquidiser and blend until smooth. For a coarser soup, use the food processor for chopping. Place the soup in the fridge and chill for about 3 hours.

Serve cold, adding a few ice cubes to the serving bowl if desired.

BEETROOT SOUP
1 onion, peeled and chopped
1 tbsp polyunsaturated oil
225g (8oz) potato, peeled and diced
450g (1lb) freshly cooked beetroot
1.25 litres (2pt) water
Salt and pepper
1 tbsp lemon juice
1 tbsp natural yogurt
2 tbsp skimmed milk

Serves 4

Fry the onion in the oil in a large saucepan until soft, then add the potatoes and cook for 5 minutes. Skin the beetroot and dice the flesh, then add to the saucepan with the water. Bring to the boil then simmer, with the lid on, for 20 minutes or until the potatoes are soft. Liquidise the soup, then return to the saucepan and season with salt, pepper and lemon juice. Reheat gently. Divide soup into four bowls. Mix the yogurt with the skimmed milk and pour over each bowl of soup before serving.

If you are hard up when you have friends coming round, a good idea is to serve a good thick soup, such as lentil soup, followed by stuffed baked potatoes. This makes a very substantial meal for very little money, and requires next to no cooking at all.

THICK LENTIL SOUP
225g (8oz) split orange lentils, washed
600ml (1pt) vegetable stock
1 medium-sized onion, peeled and chopped
1 carrot, sliced
3 cloves of garlic
½ tsp turmeric
½ tsp coriander
½ tsp cumin
Pinch of ground cumin, cloves and nutmeg
Salt and pepper
A little lemon juice
Parsley, chopped (optional)

Serves 4

Simmer the lentils gently in the vegetable stock with the chopped onion, carrot and garlic for 1–1½ hours until the lentils are soft, then drain, keeping the juices. Purée the lentils, using a little of the reserved juice. Add the spices and enough cooking liquid to make it the required consistency. Adjust the seasoning and add a generous squeeze of lemon juice.

Garnish with chopped parsley before serving.

Easy main courses for entertaining

KIDNEY AND MUSHROOM CASSEROLE
6 lambs' kidneys
15g (½oz) butter or margarine
225g (8oz) onions, peeled and chopped
600ml (1pt) stock made with a stock cube or 3 tbsp Bovril
1 tbsp tomato purée
Salt and pepper
Bay leaf
225g (8oz) carrots, peeled and sliced
225g (8oz) mushrooms, sliced
1 carton natural yogurt, small

Serves 4

Remove the skin from the kidneys, cut them in half and take out the core. (If you prefer, the butcher will always do this for you if you ask him nicely.) Fry them in heated butter until browned. Add the onions and fry gently for 5 minutes, then place in a casserole. Stir in the stock, and the tomato purée and season. Add the carrots and the mushrooms. Cover with a lid and cook at 350°F/180°C, gas mark 4 for 1½–2 hours.

Just before serving, stir in one small carton of yogurt, but do not let this boil, it will just thicken the casserole.

PORTUGUESE LIVER
450g (1lb) liver
1 clove of garlic, peeled and crushed
2 tbsp white wine vinegar
Bay leaf
A few peppercorns
15g (½oz) lard
150ml (¼pt) stock made with a stock cube
1 carton yogurt, small

Serves 4

Slice the liver, or better still get the butcher to do it for you, very thinly. Make a marinade with the garlic, vinegar, bay leaf and peppercorns and leave the liver in the marinade overnight. Drain thoroughly, reserving the marinade. Melt just enough lard in a frying pan to cover the base and, when hot, quickly fry the liver until just cooked. Keep the liver warm on a serving dish. To the pan juices add the marinade and stock blended with the yogurt. Heat gently but do not boil. Pour over the liver.

BRAISED LAMB WITH CAPERS AND YOGURT
This recipe is very quickly prepared and is excellent if you have guests. I have taken it from *Low, Slow, Delicious* cookbook by Martha Lomask (Book Club Associates), which has many other recipes very easy to prepare the day before, so there is no rush when your guests arrive.

1½kg (3lb) shoulder or half leg of lamb
150ml (¼pt) white wine or water
3 tbsp capers
1 medium onion, peeled and sliced

½ tsp dried tarragon
½ tsp dried thyme
1 dsp oil
150g (5oz) natural yogurt

Serves 6

Electric slow cooker: preheat pot on HIGH for 15 minutes

1   Trim the joint of as much fat as you can, removing the fell.
Heat the oil in a pan and brown the meat very well. Blanch the
onions for 2 minutes in boiling water and lay in the bottom of
the pot. Put in the lamb and add the herbs. Heat the wine or
water almost to boiling point and pour in. Cook on HIGH for 30
minutes, then on LOW for 7 to 8 hours.
2   Fifteen minutes before serving, take out the lamb and keep it
warm. Stir in the capers and yogurt and heat on LOW until
completely blended. You may want to remove the fat from the
cooking juices before you stir in the yogurt.

Casserole cooking: preheat oven to 400°F/200°C, gas mark 6

As in steps 1 and 2 above, but put lamb in an open casserole in
hot oven for about 25 minutes, then reduce heat to 325°F/170°C,
gas mark 3 and cover the casserole. Cook another 3 hours, then
finish with the capers and yogurt.

LEMON CHICKEN WITH CUCUMBER SAUCE
4 chicken breasts, skinned
Grated rind and juice ½ lemon
Seasoning
½ cucumber, peeled and chopped
1 tbsp honey
150ml (¼pt) natural yogurt
1 tsp dill seeds

Serves 4

Sprinkle the lemon rind over the chicken together with the
seasoning, and bake in a moderate oven 350°F/180°C, gas mark 4
for about 15 minutes. Mix the remaining ingredients together
and pour over the chicken. Cover and cook in a moderate oven
for a further 40–50 minutes.

19 'I cannot see the point of snacks.'

The aim of the Eating Plan is to get your eating back to normal permanently, and that means making changes. Stop thinking about eating just three times a day, instead think about the need to feed your body more often. Regular small meals, of suitable food, will stop you feeling hungry and cut out the urge to binge.

Weight-loss diets recommend eating three set meals a day, but that is not a normal pattern of eating. People who do not suffer from eating disorders eat more – they snatch a doughnut mid-morning, a sandwich before lunch and a chocolate bar with their afternoon tea – but unlike you, it does not worry them. There is nothing to stop you eating a healthy snack at these times instead. Compulsive eaters need to maintain their blood sugar level to stop the cravings for food. If it drops, you feel tired, moody, depressed and hungry. Eating frequent small protein-based meals and snacks is the best way to stabilise the blood sugar level. The golden rule to remember is 'Never go longer than four hours without protein'.

'I'll get fat if I eat snacks.'

Gabriella kept to the Eating Plan from Monday to Thursday, but on Friday she only had one cup of coffee all day. She said: 'I had a really good day and as I wasn't really hungry I didn't eat all day. It cheered me up because I thought about all the weight I would lose, it made me really happy. I see little point in eating when I am not really hungry, after all it makes you fat.'

The problem was that on Saturday she started bingeing at 3.30 in the morning, and by the end of the day she had eaten many times more calories than had she eaten properly the day before. Her early morning binge included half a loaf of bread and margarine, a carton of cottage cheese, a quarter pound of Cheddar cheese, two packets of digestive biscuits and a couple of tins of custard. The rest of the day she doesn't record, it was 'just one long binge'.

Compulsive eaters often allow themselves to go too long without food, which leads to bingeing. Eating three snacks a day will not allow your body to get to the stage when it craves food and you eat everything in sight. By planning your snacks each day, there should always be something healthy to eat at hand. Three snacks and three meals a day may seem a lot of food to someone who lives on cottage cheese, lettuce leaves and black coffee, but think about how much you manage to eat all at once in a binge, maybe loaves of bread, packets of biscuits, bowls of breakfast cereals and plates of cakes, at the same time making yourself feel helpless and miserable. Snacks will not make you fat, they will make you well again. Whether you are hungry or not, you must force yourself to eat three snacks a day until your eating is under control, and after that you will probably carry on eating them anyway.

'I don't have time for snacks.'

You find the time to eat mounds of buns, cakes and biscuits when you are bingeing, it takes no time at all to eat a protein snack which will not lower your blood sugar level or make you feel guilty or unhappy, as well as stopping you binge. It is up to you to find the time if you want to get your eating under control. It need only take a few minutes each morning to prepare your snacks for the day. Elizabeth said she did not have time to prepare her snacks before work, but she spent 15 minutes crimping her shoulder-length hair. We told her to get up 10 minutes earlier. Work out what is more important to you, staying in the Food Trap or changing your lifestyle in order to get well. You can plan your snacks in advance and prepare them the night before if you do find yourself in a rush in the mornings. And if you really do not have the time, simply open a tin of tuna in brine, have a yogurt, pick up a Camembert triangle and an apple or pour yourself a glass of milk.

'Snacks are boring.'

Snacks can be as boring, or as exciting, as you make them. Sticking to cottage cheese and yogurt each day will get tedious, so start experimenting and using your imagination. You can eat anything that contains protein, and that includes meat, poultry, fish, dairy produce, beans, pulses and nuts. Try celery dipped in taramasalata or cod's roe with slices of tomato on crispbread. Make tasty cheese dips to eat with raw vegetables for example, blend yogurt with Stilton cheese, fromage frais or, providing you are not watching your weight too much, avocado with low fat cream cheese.

'I am not allowed to eat at work.'

You are entitled to a break by law, stand up for yourself and make sure you take it. Ask your union representative for support or explain to your boss that your health depends on you having at least a 5 minute break. That is all the time it takes to eat a snack. It need only be a packet of peanuts. You may not be permitted to eat, but surely you are allowed to drink, a cup of decaffeinated coffee made with milk is fine, or a packet of protein powder mixed in orange juice. Remember how crafty you have become at bingeing, eating in the car, on the toilet, while someone's back is turned? Well, use your own resources and snack in the same way.

Many compulsive eaters who use this excuse admit that their workmates tuck into cakes and biscuits mid-morning. In that case, there is nothing to stop you opening up a pot of yogurt or unwrapping a piece of cheese. Your problem is that you are lacking in confidence and do not want to be 'different' from your friends, even when it comes between solving your eating problem. It may be hard to eat your savoury snack while they are eating sugary treats, especially if they are munching their doughnuts right beside you. But remember that you have an eating disorder, they do not.

'I play golf every morning and cannot eat a snack on the course.'

Carry a piece of cheese and fruit with you or keep a packet of nuts in your pocket. They will not take up much room and will not be any problem to eat during your game.

Snacks

RAINBOW CURD CHEESE
A mixture of curd cheese, chopped up, freshly cooked beetroot (most pickled beetroot has sugar in it so check the label if you are going to use this) and bean sprouts.

TINNED COD'S ROE
This can be eaten on its own or spread on a Ryvita, or mixed with hard-boiled eggs.

CELERY STUFFED WITH CHEESE
Take some low fat cheese and spread over celery sticks. Leave ready prepared in the fridge for a really speedy snack.

BEETROOT YOGURT
120ml (4fl oz) low fat natural yogurt
1 tsp Dijon mustard
1 tsp lemon juice
¼ tsp pepper
450g (1lb) cooked beetroot, diced

Makes 2 snack-size helpings

Mix the yogurt, mustard, lemon juice and pepper together and add the cooked beetroot and stir carefully. Serve hot or cold.

SMOKED SALMON COTTAGE CHEESE
50g (2oz) offcuts of smoked salmon
1 small carton of cottage cheese
Lemon juice
Black pepper

Makes 2 snacks

Put the smoked salmon, lemon juice and pepper into a blender and then add to the cottage cheese. This can be spread on to crispbreads or used as a stuffing for hard-boiled egg or tomatoes.

DEVILLED HAM WITH CELERY
225g (8oz) lean ham
50g (2oz) low fat spread

2 tsp Worcestershire sauce
2 tsp mustard
Sticks of celery

Makes 4 snack meals

Place the ham in a food processor with the low fat spread, Worcestershire sauce and mustard and blend until mixed. This will keep in a fridge for one week or in a freezer for a month. Fill celery sticks with the mixture.

TOMATO AND TUNA MIX
100g (3½oz) can of tuna in brine, drained
1 tbsp tomato purée (sugar-free)
1 carrot, grated
25g (1oz) low fat spread
Seasoning to taste

Makes 2/3 snacks

Mix all the ingredients together either by hand or in a blender. Spread on a crispbread or fill celery sticks with the mixture which will keep in the fridge for up to a week.

CURRY DIP
120ml (4fl oz) low fat plain yogurt
¼ tsp curry powder
¼ tsp lemon juice
Pinch of ground cumin
Pinch of white pepper

Makes 1/2 snacks

Mix together all the ingredients in a bowl and chill in the fridge. Serve as a dip with assorted fresh raw vegetables.

HAM SLAW MIX
Mix together ham with either ready-made or home-made low-calorie coleslaw. You can use chicken or beef as a variation.

FETA CHEESE SALAD
25g (1oz) Feta cheese, cubed
2 medium tomatoes, sliced
A few slices of cucumber

2 or 3 black olives
Lettuce
1 tbsp French dressing

Mix together the cheese, tomatoes, cucumber and olives. Sprinkle these over the lettuce leaves. Toss well in the dressing.

HERRING ROES ON TOAST
75g (3oz) herring roes
1 tsp lemon juice
1 tbsp water
Seasoning

Makes 2 snacks

Poach the herring roes in the lemon juice and water, seasoning to taste. Serve on a slice of wholemeal bread or mix with half a carton of cottage cheese.

FROMAGE FRAIS
This can either be eaten on its own, or mixed with fruit or with fish.

COTTAGE CHEESE
This can be eaten on its own, although it does tend to get very boring. For a change why not try spreading a Ryvita with marmite and putting the cottage cheese on top, and top the whole thing with sliced tomatoes. Or liven up a portion of cottage cheese with some chopped cucumber and a handful of pumpkin seeds; or perhaps a few prawns, or add nuts and sultanas.

YOGURT
This is an ideal quick, easy snack, though it can get boring on its own. Again, use your imagination and try yogurt mixed with fruit, seeds or nuts.

TOFU
This is very bland on its own, but improves considerably if sardines or tuna are mashed in to it. It can also be mixed with any type of fruit and sweetened with artificial sweetener.

SIMPLE SNACKS
A slice of ham, beef, or a couple of chicken wings.

INTERESTING LYCHEE SALAD
3 lychees, peeled and halved
2 tbsp bean sprouts
1 tbsp chopped ham
1 tbsp diced red pepper
1 tbsp mixed nuts, chopped

Makes 2 snacks

Mix all the ingredients together and sprinkle with lime juice.

CHEESE
Buy small one-portion size cheeses such as Cheddar, Camembert, Brie, etc. These can be eaten on their own or with an apple, or spread on a crispbread.

HADDOCK PÂTÉ
225g (½lb) smoked haddock
150ml (¼pt) milk
½ onion
1 bay leaf
3 peppercorns
Small carton of cottage cheese
¼ tsp anchovy essence
Pinch of cayenne pepper

Makes 6 snacks

Put the fish into a saucepan with the milk, onion, bay leaf and peppercorns and cook gently for about 10 minutes or until tender. Drain and leave to cool. Flake the fish, removing all the bones and discarding the skin. Mash with a fork and slowly add the cottage cheese and anchovy essence. Sprinkle with cayenne pepper and serve chilled with wholemeal toast or crispbread.

EGGS
Try plain hard-boiled eggs or chopping them up with ham or one rasher of crisp grilled bacon and perhaps an anchovy or a sardine.

HOT CAULIFLOWER SNACK

Use any leftover boiled cauliflower. Sprinkle it with 25g (1oz) grated cheese and toast under the grill.

BAKED APPLE

Top half a baked apple with fromage frais or yogurt and sprinkle with apple pie spice. You can bake a lot of apples previously cut in half and freeze them, and this snack can be served either hot or cold.

20 You can do it.

You *can* overcome your eating problem, if you are prepared to make changes. Time after time we hear from compulsive eaters who, although desperately unhappy with their lives, believe it is easier to stay the way they are than make the choice to change.

For example, Lorraine was a compulsive eater working in an office at an electricity board, and she hated her job. She was bored with the work, had no prospect of promotion but she refused to consider changing her job because she would lose her pension when she retired in fifteen years time. Finally she saw the light and realised her eating habits would not improve until she changed what was causing her binges. She took the chance of changing her work and she got over her eating problem. She said: 'It is better to live life to the full for the next fifteen years and lose my pension than stay the way I was, unhappy and a food addict.'

Margaret's excuse was she could not stop thinking about food. She could not take up a hobby, make friends or get a job, which would have taken her mind off food and given her life a new direction, because: 'I cannot do anything because I cannot stop thinking of food.'

We told her she had the choice to get well again or remain a compulsive eater. If she chose to get well it meant making changes and she would not know what would help until she tried it. She must make a choice and take a chance. Margaret took her first step and joined an aerobics class for one hour a week. She said: 'It may have only been an hour but for that hour I didn't think about food. It was freedom for one hour and better than nothing. The next week I went to exercise classes for four hours.' Margaret is now over her eating problem and teaches exercise classes.

Some people appear to have more problems, and therefore more excuses, to cope with than others. But it does not mean they need to remain a compulsive eater. The choice is always theirs. Joan is deaf and bulimic. Her difficulty communicating depresses her and the stress led to binges. She used her deafness as an excuse not to get over her eating problem. She told us: 'You tell me to eat more protein which to me means more calories. I would rather cut out the protein and eat chocolate, although I know it will always lead to a binge. I am sure my case is hopeless because I am deaf.' We persuaded Joan to realise that the only way to get better was to make changes in her life. She would never cure her deafness and until she accepted that she would always have an eating problem. Joan went to a training school for the deaf and discovered she had a talent for tapestry which gave new purpose to her life, and she is now eating well again.

Sally wrote to us in complete despair. She suffered from depression and her compulsive eating made her life a vicious circle of depression, binges, depression. She wrote to us: 'I have eaten so much I can hardly breathe. Tears are streaming down my face and soon I will go to bed and sleep as long as possible to get another day done with. I've given up. I'm not living, I'm existing. I sit and think about something I could do to motivate myself and there is nothing. I sit in my room all day and do nothing at all. When I go out all I want to do is go home and raid the fridge. Here I am, in tears, a tubby young woman, now totally apathetic. My life is in chaos.'

We felt Sally was one of the very few people who would benefit from drug therapy as she was a manic depressive, but she could not explain her feelings to her GP. We advised her to show her doctor the letter she sent us at the Maisner Centre which explains how she felt. She was put on medication which helped her mood swings and within a few months was a transformed personality. She told us: 'I am beginning to build my life from the ashes. I'd rather hoped that the medication may have magically solved my eating problem. Not so of course, there are no magic pills that can do that. But now I can face up to my eating problem and know I will get it under control.'

Geraldine is serving a long prison sentence and, as well as coping with the confines of jail, she became bulimic. She contacted the Maisner Centre for help after a failed attempt to commit suicide. Her meals are eaten in her cell and she found herself almost constantly eating, fantasising about food and bingeing on stodgy puddings, bread and an excessive amount of tea. She wrote to us: 'My life evolves around fasting, semi-starvation and binges. I class fasting as my salvation, it gives my throat a chance to heal up from vomiting so when I do start eating it is easier to vomit. Most binges are almost violent and the food is swallowed in lumps rather than chewed. Liquid concotions are favourite, at one time it was boxes of Complan.'

But Geraldine did not use her imprisonment as an excuse. She made the choice and began thinking positively about her eating. A few weeks after starting a postal course at the Maisner Centre she was making fine progress. She wrote: 'Something is wrong with me lately, I'm just coping too well! I'm just too happy and I've got my act together. I really should be in bits by now, well wrapped up in a vicious circle, depressed and unwashed with my cell looking like a pig-sty. I'm actually waking up earlier and not still feeling tired. Living in this wing can get really heavy sometimes. All the things you have to do just to survive is unreal at times. All the bitterness and uneasiness can get on top at times in these places. Anyhow, I'm not going to slip back now.'

Instead of sitting in her cell thinking about food, she made the choice to change her lifestyle as much as possible within the confines of prison. She started an Open University course, began exercising, painting and writing to pen friends. She is now a valuable asset at the Maisner Centre as she writes to many clients who feel their own problems are insurmountable. It gives her a purpose and she is helping others.

If Geraldine can do it, so can you. However daunting your own excuses may appear to be to overcome, we hope this book has shown it can be done. Be prepared to make changes to get well. Remember, excuses won't cure you.

Appendix I   Further Reading

The Food Trap, published by George Allen & Unwin, by Paulette
   Maisner, available from the Maisner Centre. 1985.
Fasting and Feasting, published by Fontana, by Paulette Maisner
   and Jenny Pulling, available from the Maisner Centre. 1985.
Dieting Makes You Fat, Geoffrey Cannon and Hetty Einzig, Century
   Publishing, 1983.
Body Mind and Sugar, E. M. Abrahamson MD and A. W. Pezet, Holt
   Rinehart & Winston, 1960.
Fit or Fat?, Covert Bailey, Pelham Books, 1980.
A Woman in Your Own Right, Anne Dickson, Quartet Books, 1982.
Let's Eat Right to Keep Fit, Adelle Davis, Unwin Paperbacks, 1984.
Not All in the Mind, Dr Richard Mackarness, Pan Books, 1982.
The Composition of Foods, A. A. Paul and D. A. T. Southgate, HMSO,
   1987.
Jane Brody's Nutrition Book, W. W. Norton, 1981.
Low Blood Sugar, Martin Budd, Thorsons, 1981.
The Premenstrual Syndrome, Caroline Shreeve, Thorsons, 1983.
Once a Month, Katherina Dalton, Fontana, 1978.
Release from Nervous Tension, D. H. Fink, Unwin Paperbacks, 1984.
How to Survive Anorexia, published by Muller, Blond & White, by Peter
   Lambley Ph.D available from the Maisner Centre. 1983.
Women Who Love Too Much, published by Arrow Books, by Robin
   Norwood, available from the Maisner Centre. 1986.
Coping With Bulimia, Barbara French, Thorsons, 1987.

Appendix II   Useful Addresses

The following addresses include not only support groups and associations of particular use for those with eating and related problems, but also contacts for alternative therapies, sports associations and voluntary services. In most cases the main contact address is given.

Al-anon	61 Great Dover Street, London SE1 4YE 01 403 0888
Alcoholics Anonymous	140a Tachbrook Street, London SW1 01 834 8202
Anorexic Aid	The Priory Centre, 11 Priory Road, High Wycombe, Bucks. 0494 21431
British Association of Counselling	1a Little Church Street, Rugby, Warwickshire 0788 78328/9
British Wheel of Yoga	80 Lechampton Road, Cheltenham, Gloucester, GL53 OBM 0242 52 4889
Brook Advisory Centre for Young People	233 Tottenham Court Road, London W1P 9AE 01 323 1522 01 580 2991
The Centre for Autogenic Training	15 Fitzroy Square, London W1P 5HQ 01 388 1007
Citizen's Advice Bureau Service (CAB) (Greater London	31 Wellington Street, London WC2E 7DA 01 828 7022
Community Service Volunteers	237 Pentonville Road, Islington, London N1 9NJ 01 276 6601
The Compassionate Friends (for parents who have lost a child)	2 Norden Road, Blandford, Dorset DT1 7LT 0258 52760
Consumers Association	14 Buckingham Street, London WC2N 6DS 01 893 1222
Cruse (for widows, widowers and their children)	Cruse House, 126 Sheen Road, Richmond TW9 1UR 01 940 4818/9047
Depressives Anonymous	C/C Keith Middleton, 21 The Green, Cheddersley Corbet, Worcester.
Depressives Associated	19 Merley Ways, Wimborne Minster, Dorset BH21 1QN 0202 88 3957

Drug Advisory Services Ltd	111 Cowbridge Road, East Canton, Cardiff 0222 26113
Family Planning Association	27–35 Mortimer Street, London W1A 4QW 01 636 7866
Family Welfare Association	501 Kingsland Road, Dalston, London E8 4AU 01 254 6251
Gamblers Anonymous	17–23 Blantyre Street, London SW10 01 352 3060
Gingerbread (for Single Parents)	35 Wellington Street, London WC2 01 240 0953
Institute of Family Therapy	43 New Cavendish Street, London W1M 7RG 01 935 1651
International Bacchus Organisation (charitable social organisation for young professionals 20–35)	24 Eccleston Street, London SW1
International Voluntary Services	Ceresole House, 53 Regent Street, Leicester 0533 54 1962 10 Cromwell Road, Belfast 0232 38147 1 Upper Parliament Street, Liverpool L8 1TD 051 709 6726 Charlton House, 36 Hunslet Road, Leeds LS10 1EU 05324 84453
Iyengar Yoga Institute	223a Randolph Avenue, London W9 1NL 01 624 3080
Jogging Association	Westlake Cottage, New Stead, Abbey Park, Nottingham NG15 8GE 0623 79 3496
Mental Health Foundation	8 Hallam Street, London W1N 6DH
Mothers' Action Support Team (Self-help group who aim to combat the loneliness felt by women at home)	18 The Woodlands, Linton, Cambridge
National Advisory Centre on Careers for Women	Drayton House, 30 Gordon Street, London WC1H OA 01 380 0117

National Association for Mental Health	111 Mycenae Road, London SE3 7XR 01 858 4849
National Association for Mental Health (MIND)	22 Harley Street, London W1N 2ED 01 637 0741
National Association of Women's Clubs	5 Vernon Rise, Kings Cross, London, WC1X 9EP
National Council for the Divorced and Separated	13 High Street, Little Shelford, Cambridge CB2 5ES
National Council for the Single Woman and her Dependants	29 Chilworth Mews, London W2 3RG
National Council for Voluntary Organisations	26 Bedford Square, London WC1B 3HU 01 636 4066
National Federation of Women's Institutes	39 Eccleston Street, London SW1W 9NT 01 380 0117
National Housewives Register	c/o Antoinette Feraro, 245 Warwick Road, Solihull, West Midlands B92 7AH 021 706 1101
National Marriage Guidance Council	Herbert Gray College, Little Church Street, Rugby, Warwickshire 0788 732 41
Open Door Association (Agoraphobia)	447 Pensey Road, Heswell, Merseyside.
Organisation for Parents Under Stress	26 Manor Drive, Pickering, Yorkshire Y18 8DD 0602 81 9423
Overeaters/Alcoholics Anonymous	140a Tachbrook Street, London SW1 01 834 8202
Outside London Contacts	11 Redcliffe Gardens, London SW10 01 352 9779
Patient's Association	335 Grays Inn Road, London WC1X 8PX 01 837 7241
Phobic Society	4 Cheltenham Road, Chorlton-cum-Hardy, Manchester M21 1QN 061 881 1937
Relaxation for living	Danesk, 29 Burwood Park Road, Walton-on-Thames, Surrey, KT12 5LH 0932 22 7826
Release Counselling on Legal, Social and Medical Problems related to drug taking	1 Elgin Avenue, London W9 3PR
Samaritans (for local groups check your telephone directory)	London Branch, St Stephen's Church, 39 Walbrook, London EC4N 8EP 01 626 2277

Solo Clubs (for the divorced, widowed or separated)

Room 7-8, Ruskin Chambers, 191 Corporation Street, Birmingham B4 6RY 021 236 2879

The Sports Council

70 Brompton Road, London SW3 01 388 1277

The Transcendental Meditation Centre

Royden Hall, Seven Mile Lane, East Peckham, Nr Tonbridge, Kent TN12 5NH 076 72 7271

TRANEX (Tranquilliser addiction)

2 St John's Road, Harrow, Middlesex

Voluntary Work Information Services

68 Chalton Street, London NW1 1HJ 01 388 0241

Womens Aid Federation for Battered Wives

374 Grays Inn Road, London WC1 01 837 9316

Workers Educational Association (Adult Education and Social Functions)

32 Tavistock Square, London WC1 0232 49041

Index